Dogs, Jobs a
By Micha(

Forward by Rodger Savill

For many years I have served in the ministry of working with traumatized people, in particular, childhood abuse survivors. Daily I walk into people's broken and shattered hearts and lives, feeling their pain and debilitating agony caused by the terror of abuse. The tears they have shed are generated from fear against the unpredictability of the human heart.

When God formed and shaped Adam, He set the task of naming each and every living creature (Gen.2:19-20). This experience and responsibility brought Adam to his reality, that although he could have a friendship with an animal, for example, a dog, it was at the dog's level, and not at his potential and capacity for relationship and needed intimacy. It wasn't until Adam discovered this, that he was ready to understand and apply a growing maturity of sensitivity to his counterpart - Eve.

When we are not loved as we were intended to be, we experience the horror of our vulnerability in unsafe and unpredictable relationships. This vulnerability is experienced as fear, from not being able to interrupt or manage connection safely, so that over time we come to 'mistrust' the hearts of others, needing to prevent them from getting too close.

The tragedy is that the fundamental need for intimacy is turned into finding something that has a very limited need and no capacity for a deeper connection. So any living creature that merely responds to human attention, has the attraction to replace healthy heart to heart relationships and consequently becomes a safe and viable option of managed and controlled friendship or companionship.

In this place of fear, the wounded soul withdraws into itself and shrinks down to the capacity of the mammal, bird, or fish's reality and limitations. The broken heart's ability to trust intimacy has been reduced to meet their spectrum of connection. Trust is not required in an obsessive connection with pets, hearts can remain shut-down and unavailable, thus a minimized and reduced connection appears to offer heart safety.

Here is the line between enjoying what God has given us as opposed to living life through them. Animal relationships were never intended to replace our primary need for connection with God, and then with fellow humans, and in particular, intimate relationships. Being resourced in a safe and intimate relationship with our Creator enables us to gift His compassion, love, and grace to others in safe and stable ways so that we are blessed in return.

I certainly understand the innocence of the 'cross-over' in a very desperate effort to minimize the pain of trauma, and loneliness. Many, if not all of these deeply traumatized people that God has brought into the ministry for healing, have sunken so deeply into fear of relationships with fellow humans, yet the need for meaningful connection has remained so powerful, they have personified and almost deified a pet to the point of resourcing their entire life and heart needs from the poor pets limited reality.

Only sincere and open connections with fellow humans can affirm the beauty of our image and likeness we possess of our creator, therefore restoring the heart for meaningful and safe relationships. This is essential in the development and growth of discovering who, what, how and why we are, with Jesus' confidence and joy. Experiencing why we are so 'precious' to Him and knowing what He loves about us deeply establishes the confidence for our own reality in the stability of His joy.

Having run residential recovery programs over many years for childhood abuse survivors, we did have a variety of animals. However, contrary to common secular thinking, their benefit for a truly successful recovery and restoration was very limited.

Although they gained a sense of peace and comfort from the unassuming nature of the animals, which to begin with was soothing for them, the pets did, in fact, inhibit the recovery of the healing of their hearts. We observed a tendency for the traumatized individual to recess back into a fantasy of exclusive friendship/relationship with the animal, particularly when limitations of 'trust' were reached, and fear against intimacy took over.

Wounds create fear, fear gives birth to anger, anger requires addictions and obsessions to keep the heart shutdown and unavailable. When we arrive at this place – Satan wins! Mistrust of intimacy is the foundation of living as a victim, and victimization robs us of being free and the ability to celebrate the potential of our uniqueness with others.

Our problem is not that we attempt to meet and fulfill the needs of our thirsty hearts, but that we are turning to all the wrong places and things to fill them. Life is too precious to be content with awareness and reality that is merely reduced to that of a non-spiritual creature. As you read this book, don't be afraid to share with Jesus Christ your pain and seek the wonderful healing from God through Him. Listen to the heart of the writer, and let Jesus Christ start a process into wholeness and newness - now and forever!

Rodger P. Savill

Oasis Life Recovery Trust, New Zealand

Introduction:

Love Thy Neighbor, or
Love Thy Dog as Thyself?

Zoolatry
[zoh-ol-uh-tree] noun

the worship of or excessive attention to animals.

"There is a way which seems right to a man, But its end is the way of death." -Proverbs 14:12 NASB

In time memories fade, senses numb
One forgets how it feels to have loved completely
Love well young man, while you still can
Once your leaves turn, you won't love again
Is it special when you're lonely?
Will you spend your whole life
In a studio apartment with a cat for a wife?
The seasons, when they call you, do you barricade the door?
Are you stubborn, stubborn, stubborn to the core?
Is it your way, or the highway?
-David Bazan

     In the summer of 2009 the company I worked for went out of business along with many others as the economy fell into a massive recession. Over the past year I had put my heart and soul into a startup venture, working my way up from a small cubicle to a large executive office next door to the CEO.

     Losing everything was devastating, especially after all those big dreams and long hours. Everything that we built up slowly over time came tumbling down overnight, and a hope deferred made my heart sick. So I took some time off and enrolled in Bible college at CFNI in Dallas Texas. That experience helped inspire my first book, *Jesus Is My*

Bartender.

The economy was in shambles, so instead of chasing down another high-stress career position, I decided to take a brief detour while I waited to see how quickly the economy would rebound. I applied to become a certified dog trainer at a big box pet store because I've always enjoyed being around animals. I knew it would be a low stress position and that's just what I needed. I won't mention the name of the company, but they're a major player in the industry.

Dog training didn't turn into a career, but that's Ok. I was able to slow down for a while and devote more time the Lord. I learned a lot during this season of rest and I'm grateful for the experience. I began to study the Bible and pray more than ever before.

It felt like God was rewarding my decision to take a step back and seek His will. I didn't realize just how much I needed to recalibrate and heal from the past. There were a lot of ups and downs in those first thirty years at a rapid pace that was unhealthy and unsustainable.

Working at the pet store was mostly pleasant and rewarding, the dog owners who signed up for our classes were usually ambitious young professionals with busy lives. Their cute little puppies were getting bigger and harder to control every day. Our class would often turn into therapy sessions for people and we also happened to teach their dogs to obey a few basic commands.

The pet store was fun and more physically active compared to my previous desk job, but I must admit that it wasn't what I had envisioned. That's often the case with the Lord, we sign up for one thing and the Holy Spirit leads us on an unexpected adventure.

For starters, our training classes would be nearly empty if we failed to find customers during our downtime. We had to work hard in between classes or else we would only have one or two clients and our pay plan was a small base plus commission. Dog training was enjoyable, but at the end of the day, it was essentially a sales job.

We had to find our own clients, teach the classes, plus set up and clean up after class. It turned out to be two jobs for the price of one, low paying job. I do enjoy working in an entrepreneurial setting, but you'd have to start your own school if you wanted a livable income. As it turns out, God didn't bring me there for the money. His purpose for this season of my life ended up being a crash course in humanity.

"The steps of a man are established by the LORD, when he delights in his way;" -Psalm 37:23 ESV

At the end of the day, working only forty hours each week felt like semi-retirement compared to the never-ending grind of my previous positions. Dog training in a place like this attracts a lot of young, aspiring college students and retired folks who are looking to supplement their income because they receive social security or a pension from somewhere else.

Entry-level positions like this provide an easy way to get a foot in the door if you're new to the industry and eager to learn. The big box stores do offer paid training, which is nice, and plenty of networking opportunities. If a low paying job leads you to a career in dog training or helps you pay for college, then it's a win-win for everyone.

While I was there I watched thousands of wealthy pet owners walk through our doors. I will never forget those exasperated pet owners who had bit off more than they could chew with a blue-eyed Husky or a scruffy mutt from the animal shelter. The pet store was filled with animal lovers from all walks of life. For some it was a hobby, for others, it was an obsession.

At one point, during my first few weeks I prayed that God would help me understand the absurdity of it all. Some of the people I met were absolutely crazy about their animals, and for some reason it really rubbed me the wrong way. At that moment I felt a strong impression that much of what I had witnessed was idolatry. I didn't fully understand idolatry at the time, so I began to study and after a few years, that research led to the completion of this book. I hope you find it both entertaining and insightful.

The best part of my search happened when God helped me overcome idolatry in my own life. It started with opening my eyes and being more honest with myself. As I dug deeper, I was able to see how much He has done in my life, even when I was a little boy. Those who seek the Lord earnestly will find Him.

I could fill an entire book with stories of divine appointments that were surely orchestrated by the kindness of God. This study has been a real eye-opener for me, and now I'm pleased to share the fruit of my labor with you. I wish I could thank everyone I've met along the way, and I hope you grow closer to the Lord today.

Michael Mistretta
Moravian Falls, North Carolina

Chapter 1

My victory over idolatry

"The heart of the Gospel is change. It is transformation. It is being born again into a new life... A real encounter with God means change." -David Wilkerson

"And if it is evil in your eyes to serve the Lord, choose this day whom you will serve, whether the gods your fathers served in the region beyond the River, or the gods of the

Amorites in whose land you dwell. But as for me and my house, we will serve the Lord." -Joshua 24:15 ESV

Before we begin I'd like to share a bit about my testimony. If I can overcome the bondage of idolatry then no one is beyond hope. The freedom we have in Christ is a personal guarantee from God that if we walk with Him then we can walk away from our self-imposed prison. A heart of pride says "my problems are too big for God" because He is ready, willing, and able to help you right now.

This is the ministry of reconciliation, which is important to me because I was a slave to a host of worthless idols for years. God set me free when I repented and now I am walking in victory. From what I've seen, the hardest obstacle to overcome (besides pride) is our excuses. When you are willing to lay down your pride and your excuses, the act of giving up idolatry is the easy part.

My testimony is proof of God's goodness, and sometimes I don't know whether to laugh or cry when people try to tell me what God can't do. Television was my first idol and it all started when I was around 12 years old. The TV and computer screen became a virtual babysitter that devoured countless hours of my life.

It kept me isolated from friends and family for years, but when I was a little boy I didn't watch much TV. When I was growing up we lived in a rural area outside of Lawrence Kansas. We had 20 acres of land and a beautiful home at the top of a hill with a nice view of the Kaw Valley.

As kids, our parents would often tell us to go outside and play. We ran around barefoot on gravel roads all summer and went sledding in the winter. The TV in our house had an analog 'rabbit ear' antenna that struggled to pick up four or five fuzzy channels on a clear day. Cable TV wasn't available in our area and satellite TV was still prohibitively expensive. On most days zoning out in front of the TV was not a big temptation.

I might watch a couple of cartoons after school or on Saturday morning, and we rented movies once in a while on the weekends. When we went to a movie theater it was a big deal. Most of my free time was spent drawing at the dining room table or playing outside. I loved to explore the woods that surrounded our home and wade through the creek at the bottom of our hill.

We rode bikes, shot BB guns, and jumped on our trampoline far more than we watched TV. I played little league baseball and in the spring we would plant a sizable vegetable garden that produced an abundance of corn, green beans, peppers, tomatoes, and watermelons. We also planted an orchard with apple, cherry, peach, pear, and plum trees. The garden required a good deal of hard work in the summer heat, but it was fun at times and it helped me develop a strong work ethic.

Those carefree days came to an abrupt end when my mother and stepfather separated and divorced. I was halfway through the sixth grade when my mother and I moved into town. That's when things took a turn for the worse. By this point I had already changed schools a handful of times due to the marital woes in my family.

My brother and sister went to live with my Father a few miles away and my mom took a full-time job at the University of Kansas. I was the youngest of my siblings and no one stopped to ask my opinion. Within a month everything settled down and we installed cable TV at our new apartment. For aw while I lived like an only child with minimal supervision.

Moving meant losing my friends, and I had the experience of being home alone for the first time. My new daily routine consisted of turning on the TV after school and playing video games until my mom came home from work around 5 pm. Within a year I had unfettered access to a desktop computer with AOL Internet service.

These were the early days of the Internet and I could search online for almost anything and chat with strangers without supervision. I was hooked instantly. I'd log onto the computer right after school and sometimes stay online until midnight or later with only a break for dinner and a couple of TV shows. I rarely opened my backpack or did any homework in those days.

Life could have been worse if not for Wednesday night youth group, which quickly became the highlight of my week. During that time we transitioned away from a traditional mainline church and started going to a nondenominational, spirit-filled church. Even as a child you could feel the difference.

My experience in church went from boring and dry to fun and fascinating. I played the drums in our youth band and did vocals too. We had a great youth pastor named Mike McMenomey and a wonderful worship leader, Randy Wilkens Those two men invested a lot of time and energy into my life and I am extremely grateful for their dedication to the ministry.

During the summer after 7th grade, my mother let me go to summer camp with my youth group. I didn't know it yet, but my new routine of watching TV all the time was about to be interrupted by the very hand of God. Our group drove a few old Chevy vans down from Kansas to Christ for The Nations Institute in Dallas Texas. The camp was called Youth For The Nations.

A few days into the camp I heard a clear and powerful presentation of the Gospel during an evening session in the main auditorium. The speaker gave an invitation for us to stand and respond to his message. I came to the front, said a prayer of faith, and committed my life to the Lord. The next evening there was another speaker with another message. When I responded to the altar call that night I was filled with the Holy Spirit, it was amazing beyond words.

I grew up in church but everything changed that night

in Texas. Now it was personal, and I knew without a doubt that God loved me. I felt the presence of the Lord so strongly that it could only be described in superlatives. The sensation was beautiful, it was like a warm flow of liquid electricity, followed by a refreshing blast of joy and peace like I'd never felt before. That same joy is still with me today.

Without realizing it, God instantly broke off hindrances and healed deep wounds in my heart. It was the best week of my life. I didn't understand at the time, but this was an Acts chapter 2 experience. I felt euphoric and light-headed, but I was not drunk (nor emotionally manipulated) as some might suppose. No, this was transformational and long-lasting. I had a big goofy smile on my face for days afterward, and I can't help but smile whenever I think about what the Lord did that day.

"For to everyone who has, more shall be given, and he will have an abundance; but from the one who does not have, even what he does have shall be taken away." -Matthew 25:29 NASB

When I came home from summer camp, my mother promptly sent me to a weekend youth retreat in Topeka Kansas where I experienced the love of Christ more than before and spent hours soaking in His presence. God was laying down His foundation inside my heart. A few days later my mom and I went to a conference at Metro Vineyard Fellowship in Kansas City. This was 1993 and a Charismatic renewal that started at a church called the Toronto Airport Vineyard. Revival was in full swing and it was absolutely incredible. People were traveling from around the world to experience the revival.

We had a great time that week and seriously considered moving to Kansas City. Instead of moving, we drove there from Lawrence every Sunday but we weren't bothered by the one hour commute each way. It was a small price to pay for something that money could never buy. The incredible experiences and wonderful people we met and were easily worth the drive.

My mother and I would listen to worship music and talked about everything on those drives that never felt long. The revival made us hungry for the power of God and He never let us down. The whole place was overflowing with love and kindness. I had read parts of the Bible before but now I started reading the Bible with a hunger that I had never known.

Before we left the conference I was invited to join Metro's youth group at an upcoming weekend event called *Acquire the Fire*. When I got there I was surprised to see thousands of young adults who were passionate about Jesus. We had a great time and I didn't want to go home. At each event I met teenagers and adults who were kind and mature beyond their years.

Nearly everyone seemed to love the Lord with a zeal that I had never experienced. Their smiles were warm and genuine, the people I met weren't striving or putting on a show. We spoke with visitors from Europe, Africa, Russia, Asia, Australia and South America. That summer was a real melting pot, people came from different denominational backgrounds, it wasn't just a bunch of reformed baptists or evangelicals together in one place. That's what you'd expect from most religious conferences or seminars.

I met former Catholics, Mennonites and recent converts who came out of witchcraft and atheism. The nondenominational movement wasn't intended to be a new denomination, (although that has happened to some degree) it was birthed for the sake of unity, freedom, clarity, and a humble pursuit of Biblical orthodoxy. It wasn't perfect but a lot of good came out of those early efforts.

That summer drastically changed the course of my life. Words cannot describe the sweet presence of the Lord but this verse is fitting: "Many waters cannot quench love,

Nor will rivers overflow it; If a man were to give all the riches of his house for love, It would be utterly despised.'" - Song of Solomon 8:7

After an unforgettable summer, I went home to my Dad's house. At this point I was splitting time between there and my mom's apartment, but that's another story for another day. That day I sat down on the couch, and turned on the TV, which had been my usual routine. A few moments later, something inside of me felt uneasy. Here were the same loud, obnoxious TV commercials I'd seen a million times before, but now it was grievously offensive. My heart was shouting, "how stupid do they think I am?"

My eyes were opened as if it were the first time, it was like scales fell from the eyes of my heart. It felt like a spell was broken, and suddenly my head pounded with the throbs of a nasty headache. That was odd because even now I hardly ever have headaches. A powerful conviction came over me along with a higher level of sensitivity to the Holy Spirit.

"He who has ears to hear, let him hear." -Matthew 11:15 ESV

After a few moments I picked up the remote and turned off the TV. My headache went away instantly. The whole experience lasted less than thirty seconds, but the impact was permanent. After a few moments of silence, I felt a strong impression of what was happening in the unseen spiritual world. Just to be clear, I wasn't being religious or stuck up, no, this was a purely visceral experience.

What I felt was incredibly jarring and I kept it to myself for a long time. I don't recall anyone speaking out against Television specifically. No one put this idea into my head (which is exactly what my critics will claim). In reality, most of the people around me were head over heels in a pursuit of Jesus Christ. It was the kindness of God that led me to repentance, not a long list of rules and regulations.

It would be a long time before I heard a pastor speak against the mainstream media or Hollywood. Much to my chagrin, millions of Christians today are content to waste their potential in front of a TV. If you count up all the hours of TV time that Americans view in their lifetime, the grand total easily adds up to 9 or 10 years.

All of a sudden I was thinking about better things to do with my time. God pulled me away from the pig trough like the Prodigal Son and invited me to walk on the path of righteousness and maturity that leads to His eternal home. Despite all my failures, this experience has stuck with me. It was undoubtably the grace of God and a clear answer to specific prayers. "When I was a child, I spoke like a child, I thought like a child, I reasoned like a child. When I became a man, I gave up childish ways." - 1 Corinthians 13:11 ESV

In ancient cultures there was no such thing as being a teenager, you were either a child or an adult. That isn't to say that someone is fully mature but that they've made a firm decision to become a man and stop behaving like a boy.

I decided to follow Jesus with the faith of a child, but after that moment I knew it was time to grow up. It's a process and those years were the start of a great adventure that still makes me feel like a pioneer on a good day. I still got in trouble as a young adult and felt rebellious at times, but I was making a serious effort to stay on the narrow path (which isn't true for anyone who's still acting like Peter Pan well into their twenties or thirties).

On my birthday in August, I received a wonderful gift from my mother. Thanks to her I traded my Children's Bible for a premium leather-bound Bible. I loved that Bible and still have it today. At one point, I left in a coffee shop and thought it was gone forever. We bought a replacement Bible a few weeks later. About two years later, someone walked up to me in school and returned the Bible I had lost. I was so happy to have it back.

That happened during a rough time during my junior year of high school, and it felt like a miracle. I accepted it as a sign of God's redemption, restoration, and grace. I've made a lot of mistakes since the summer of '93, but I'm still holding on to the love that I discovered back then. Some of my best accomplishments came as a direct result of turning off the TV.

That would not have been possible without the power of Christ. Plenty of character-building comes from sports, music, ministry, and friendships. Most of that would have been nonexistent if I was still stuck in the world's matrix of mindless entertainment.

During my teenage years I developed a passion for reading and writing that's still producing good fruit today. This book wouldn't have been possible if I hadn't said no to all kinds of "permissible, but not beneficial" opportunities. Today, my goal is to spend more time creating and less time consuming, but I'd be lying if I said I never struggled against the temptation of idolatry.

After the summer of 1993, my mother and I attended Metro Vineyard Fellowship in Grandview Missouri every Sunday morning for years. It was a large, vibrant ministry hub that would eventually become IHOP, the International House of Prayer in Kansas City. Our church building was an old Ice Hockey arena that had been converted into a church. Thirty years later, it looks more or less the same. I will never forget the wonderful people and amazing music that came out of the Vineyard movement in the 90s.

Even so, the long commute had a few drawbacks. Living in one city, while attending church in another made it hard to develop deep friendships. If anything, I wish we would have just moved there permanently. Instead, we split our time which was challenging at times. I didn't mind the drive, but I was often disappointed when someone invited me to a birthday party or even a Friday night hang out in Kansas City. I couldn't go most of the time because it was an hour away.

We made the most of our situation and I am eternally grateful for those years. In all my travels, I've never seen a large group of pastors, evangelists, intercessors, and worship leaders working together in close proximity each day with such a high level of humility and unity. Nearly everyone I've met there demonstrated a high level of integrity to match their professional abilities.

I visit IHOP's prayer room whenever I'm in the area, and I met my wife at IHOP when I was living in Kansas City in the summer of 2013. I listen to IHOP's 24/7 Livestream almost every day with their free mobile app (or on Youtube). Their prayer meeting is unique because the music hasn't stopped since 1999.

The production itself is seamless, as soon as one worship team finishes a set, another team begins. Sometimes I leave it on in the background all day while I'm working, or at night if I'm having trouble sleeping. If you haven't visited IHOP's Global Prayer Room, I would encourage you to plan a trip to go in person and visit them online right now.

Just stop and soak in the presence of the Lord for an hour or two, you won't be disappointed. The power that flows from the prayer room is peaceful and relaxing, but at times the rapid-fire prayer and intercession is intense. It all depends on the leader and the situation. They pray over current events and the music constantly varies. If you stick around long enough, you'll see there's something for everyone.

If you've never prayed or worshipped for an hour straight, that's OK, you can build up to it over time. Think of it like you're going to the gym for the first time (or the first time in a long time). The prayer and worship leaders are like personal trainers who work to encourage and motivate you. If you want to be like the persistent widow that Jesus praised in Luke chapter 18, you've got to start where you are right now.

"will not God bring about justice for His elect who cry to

Him day and night, and will He delay long over them?" - Luke 18:7 NASB

Chapter 2

Sheep without a shepherd

"For if you were to have countless tutors in Christ, yet you would not have many fathers..."
-1 Corinthians 4:15 NASB

"Many pastors criticize me for taking the Gospel so seriously. But do they really think that on Judgment Day, Christ will chastise me, saying, `Leonard, you took Me too seriously´?"
-Leonard Ravenhill

Many of my best memories have been in church. That's hard for some to understand, but it's my experience and it can be yours too. I'm grateful for the charismatic revival in the 90s, and God knows I must have needed it for the calling He placed on my life. It's more than just fond memories, I still carry that fire with me.

My early years at home were rough, but some of that was my fault. Besides, there's nothing to gain by playing the blame game. In spite of what the self-help gurus say, real

Christians know that Jesus never promised to take away all our problems. (Matthew 10:34)

The Lord gives us the grace to endure, and plenty of gifts to remind us of His great favor. We should use those to help pull others from the pit of despair because for some, life is like a prison. My parents each went through two messy divorces before I graduated high school. I've had two step-dads, two step-moms, and I attended five different elementary schools.

It was a bumpy ride to say the least, but His love sustained me through those times of suffering and grief. No matter what happened, I never lost my joy. When I found Jesus I started singing and playing a variety of musical instruments. I joined the youth band at a local church in my hometown and started training on the drums, guitar, and vocals. God blessed those early efforts, and music was a huge relief from the stress of school and family life.

Making music and singing was a lot of fun, but that also brought more temptations my way. I worked diligently on my craft, and that led to bigger shows and bigger mistakes. Around the age of sixteen, I was invited to work with a team of professionals in the Christian music industry. What started out as an exciting opportunity quickly devolved into a stressful mess.

I won't call anyone out by name, but that year marked my first experience with the ugly side of Christianity as a business. The producers, engineers, and promoters didn't seem to care about me or my personal life. In my opinion they only cared about our performance on stage and in the studio. The leaders were outwardly friendly, but you'd never hear a word from them unless they needed something.

The producers showered me with compliments in the early days, but the whole experience felt superficial and staged (even when we were off-stage). After a while, if you made any mistake in rehearsals, or in the studio, tempers would flare. That's when I realized this was a business above all else.

I was working overtime with voice lessons and I joined my school's choir to improve my skills. The ministry executives who promoted my band may have started with good intentions at some point, but in practice they put a ton of pressure on a group of teenage volunteers and called it a ministry.

"Then said Jesus, Father, forgive them; for they know not what they do." -Luke 23:34 KJV

My home life became increasingly unstable during this time, which interfered with my focus. During this time I wasn't doing much to build up my relationship with the Lord and no was really encouraging me to do much beyond going to church and attending church events. Christianity was now being reduced to a spectator sport, which felt incredibly stifling after all I'd experienced in the revival.

We played in front of a thousand people or more nearly every week. We headlined shows at theme parks and opened up big events for Jars of Clay, Jennifer Knapp, Kirk Franklin, Delirious, Third Day, Geoff Moore and other well-known Christian bands. When the novelty and excitement wore off I started to feel empty inside. I was still praying and reading my Bible, but I didn't have close Christian friends or mentors to hold me accountable. My fellowship became superficial.

My long commute to band practice was an hour each way and by this point I was almost driving everywhere by myself. I was alone during most of my free time. I started sleeping with my girlfriend and with all the pain in my life it was my escape. I didn't want to be alone. Whenever I wasn't with my girlfriend, all my efforts went into music and socializing to avoid being at home with my parents. They were both in a rough place emotionally and I had a hard time getting along with them. So I was forced to bounce back and forth between living at my mom's or dad's about ten times or more during high school.

One day during a stressful band practice, I had failed to memorize a few of the lyrics for one of my songs and I was immediately dropped by my producers. Easy come, easy go. The dismissal itself was brief, cold and entirely devoid of emotion. I never spoke to anyone in that organization after that day. It was a whirlwind of excitement that lasted about a year, but it took me nearly a decade to forgive the shortsighted ministry leaders who could not have cared less about my heart.

Since then, I've met dozens of professional musicians who felt used and had similar experiences in places like Nashville and Hollywood. The Christian music industry treated me like a product and it was always a one way relationship.

They expect you to drop everything and give it your all, and that's what we did. I was able to work with a group of incredibly talented musicians, and I'm grateful for those moments. In return for my efforts, I got a bit of experience on the stage and in the studio. I enjoyed the limelight and the roar of the crowd, but a deep root of bitterness crept into my life during that time. I believe that's mainly due to a lack of deep, meaningful fellowship and the accountability that comes from discipleship.

The pursuit of music as a career is costly. During high school I worked a part-time job to fund my music. My parents gave me a car and helped in other ways too. It was fun but I can only imagine how great it would have been with mentors and friends who were closer than a brother. The leaders in my music ministry could have called me once a week or taken me out for coffee to talk about life, but that never happened. I really did look up to those guys and even a small amount of help would have meant the world to me.

After that, I sang and led worship for several other worship groups but I didn't accomplish much. I started going to more secular concerts and continued to have sex with my girlfriends. I made plenty of foolish choices during that time, but the worst was yet to come. The Bible says sin is fun for a season, (Hebrews 11:25) but as any mature believer can attest, the hangover can be brutal.

I gave up on the Christian music industry before graduating high school and abruptly shifted my time to working and playing at dive bars, night clubs, and music festivals. When I graduated from high school I moved to a suburb of Kansas to attend a community college. Without any Christian influences I started smoking pot, experimenting with other drugs, and drinking at parties for the first time. I would occasionally DJ and bartend private parties while I pursued secular music.

I took a full-time job selling mattresses at a furniture company and went to school part-time. Since it was a retail job I had to work every Saturday and Sunday. In retrospect, I realize that I could have attended an early church service on Sunday or Saturday evening, but that never happened. The callouses on my heart formed slowly and silently. I made no efforts to find a local church and I slowly drifted away from my friends at IHOP (which was still about a half hour away from school and work).

I started smoking weed and spending more time with my girlfriend and our smoking buddies from work and school. We were night owls and stayed up most nights hanging out smoking and listening to music. I never made a conscious decision to drift away from the Lord, it just happened gradually over time. All I cared about back then was sex, drugs, and rock n' roll.

There wasn't an angsty moment of teenage rage or a dramatic rejection of God. I simply refused to do what was right. My faith and devotion faded into a memory, like dust settling on a bookshelf. During those years, I had a reputation for being alive, but spiritually, I was dead. To make matters worse, I didn't know how to cook or take care of myself. I squandered most of my time getting stoned and I gave up on college.

By this point I wasn't making any real progress in music because I was more concerned with the party life. Nearly four years would pass before I stumbled back into a church like the Prodigal Son. I am grateful to my big sister who moved to Kansas City when I was 23 and helped me find a decent church in our area. She also taught me a variety of useful life skills and cared enough to ask sharp questions and challenge some of my foolish assumptions.

Church attendance was a good start, but I needed serious help. Unfortunately that wouldn't materialize for another six years. In the meantime, I cut back on the parties considerably but I still occasionally sought out comfort in sex and smoking.

You can blame me for everything if that makes you feel better, but shirking away from ministry opportunities by refusing to help others isn't exactly the hallmark of Christian maturity. Wouldn't it be nice if someone like you would have showed up and stuck around long enough to pull me out of my dungeon? I'm OK now, that's not the point. This book is about what we can do right now to help those who are less fortunate.

I think it's unhelpful to assume that people like me should be expected to know and obey everything that you've learned. My worst critics generally tend to be people who didn't have a rough past so they can't relate. They have been forgiven little and love little. (Luke 7:47)

If you had a somewhat peaceful childhood then it's hard to have empathy for people who stumble with things that aren't a problem for them. You've never had a drinking problem, sure, but you likely struggle with other, equally evil issues. Maybe it's malicious slander, bitter resentment, or petty gossip. I can assure you that those sins are just as destructive as the worst bouts of alcoholism.

I had to face the consequences of my bad choices, as

we all do. Those were my sins of "commission" but I hope others will recognize their sins of "omission" and that's the good they were supposed to do. (James 4:7)

I feel like I love much because I have been forgiven much. If you had a boring, sheltered, or even an uneventful childhood, then consider yourself lucky. I take full responsibility for my choices, but everything happened so quickly when I was young. When I move to a new town for college, my spiritual covering was significantly diminished. I should have gone to some kind of Bible college straight away or found a place to live near IHOP.

I moved to a big city without a spiritual covering. It was hard to balance work, school, friends, and music. Through work and music I met tons of successful Christians during that time, but I failed in my attempts to develop a connection with older, mature believers. I saw brief glimpses of happy, healthy marriages, and I desperately wanted to spend time with those families. Yes, I realize that none of them were perfect, but after what I'd been through, they were a breath of fresh air. You could feel it when you walked into the house, there was a clear sense of peace that rested on those homes.

So I resigned myself to hanging out with other blind guides. I frittered away my time with other kids around my age who were fond of the same bad habits. We wasted our money on drugs and booze and didn't save anything for the future. It was tragic but at the time it was better than being alone. I stumbled through my early twenties making rookie mistakes while the good people next door were busy watching TV and feeding steak to their dogs.

I wasn't anti-social or unfriendly, in fact, I had a good job and was a top performer at work. I regularly won sales contests and that was mostly due to my social skills and work ethic. Americans take pride in their rugged individualism but we seem to forget that pride is a sin and self-reliance is a myth. What I learned during that time is that the relentless pursuit of money leaves little room for anything else.

The good Lord saw all of this and helped me find a way when there seemed to be no way. The business world became the silver lining on the stormy clouds, but it was mostly nonbelievers who turned into friends. I realize now that those were ministry opportunities that I squandered. Thanks to God I found a community among my peers that I never expected.

At every stage in my career, I've been fortunate to work with business leaders who went out of their way to help me get ahead. I couldn't find a spiritual mentor to save my life, but I could always find a few men who would work alongside me and they paved the way for my success. Most of them never said a word about Jesus, but they invested tons of time into me.

Once again, the majority of those businessmen were either non-Christian or silent about their faith, but they set aside large chunks of time to help me develop practical life skills. They really did care about me even if their motives were less than pure. I don't think anyone has entirely noble motives in this day and age, but we should still resist the temptation to take advantage.

After finding my groove in sales and marketing, I went through a ten year period that felt like an endless stream of lunch meetings, business conferences, and other events. It felt so nice to find something that I could do well. I received business mentoring from incredible men who groomed me for leadership.

As a result, opportunities started to open up rapidly and I started to enjoy the adventure more and more. I was treated as an equal and it felt wonderful. All of a sudden, successful people were asking me to join them at a coffee shop and offering to pick up the tab. For me, an easy path to sobriety and contentment came from a hard day's work with a good team. Success didn't come from white knuckle willpower, or trying to avoid sin, or beating myself up when I made a mistake. It came from a commitment to hard work with (deeply flawed) people who cared about me as a person.

"But since you excel in everything--in faith, in speech, in knowledge, in complete earnestness and in the love we have kindled in you --see that you also excel in this grace of giving. I am not commanding you, but I want to test the sincerity of your love by comparing it with the earnestness of others."
-2 Corinthians 8:7 NIV

"When a man becomes a Christian, he becomes industrious, trustworthy and prosperous. Now, if that man when he gets all he can and saves all he can, does not give all he can, I have more hope for Judas Iscariot than for that man!" -John Wesley

Those early efforts are what led me to start doing freelance consulting work. It basically fell into my lap and I felt like God was guiding my path. I went from working in retail stores and call centers to advising big shot hedge fund managers and small business owners around the world. This sudden change allowed me to meet more successful Christian businessmen, and some of those introductions absolutely felt like divine appointments. Unfortunately, nothing came of that either.

Obviously, you can't develop a deep and meaningful relationship with every cool Christian that you meet along the way, but for all my business connections I couldn't find one mentor who wanted to sit down and talk about Jesus once in a while. If I couldn't (or wouldn't) directly assist with what they were pursuing, there was rarely a second meeting. I was striking out every time.

The outwardly successful Christians in my life talked a good game about faith, but most of them were devoted to the pursuit of wealth above all else. For most of them, money (greed) was their god just as much as smoking and drinking and sex (carnal pleasures) had become an idol for me.

Some of these men sat on the board of charitable organizations and routinely went on exotic mission trips, but if you weren't willing to shell out the money and join those expensive mission trips you would never join their inner circle. It played out the same way a hundred times or more during my twenties.

I would meet someone at a business conference or a seminar, and then the next day we'd go out for lunch or a cup of coffee. They were always friendly and inquisitive, that is until I politely declined whatever it was they were pitching. Then, all of a sudden, they would disconnect emotionally and turn off like a light switch. For the most part I'd never hear from them again.

I've had similar experiences with pastors and ministry leaders too. I don't mind helping people with short term projects, but if I'm going to join any business or ministry that requires a significant commitment of time, I want to get to know the people I will be working with as much as possible first. In general, if they won't make time to build a relationship, then I won't partner with them.

The Christian men who wanted me to join their group or work for them might call or text me a few times afterward, just to try and pitch me again, but nothing else. I wanted to find a few real friends to study the Bible and fellowship with but all that frantic greed (and a general fear of intimacy) prevented most of them from becoming friends with me.

Let me be clear, right now I'm talking about people who sounded like they were on fire for God when I met them. I wasn't proselytizing anyone, I wasn't begging, pleading, or misleading about my intentions. These are people who had expressed interest in working with me and getting to know me better. Job offers and business opportunities are flattering, and I'm grateful for every invitation I receive, but what I wanted was Christ-centered friendships and I often said as much upfront. Dozens of those businessmen would hold that back as bait. Without saying it they were implying that, "if you do business with me I'll do Christian activities with you".

Now that I've grown up a bit I realize it's important to strongly insist on a few of my personal convictions. Unless God points me in a specific direction, and that does happen, I will only do business with people who I connect with on a personal level. I'm not looking for best friends or anything like that, but a real connection usually takes time, and that's OK. Anyone can fake it for a day or two, but real Christians know each other after the spirit. In general, posers can only hide their true intentions for so long before their mouth speaks from the overflow of their heart.

Guys, I've been hit up for every kind of network marketing company at least once or twice. When I'm out and about, it can happen several times in a day. After a while, if you aren't careful to guard your heart, you'll feel like a piece of meat with zero value beyond your ability to close deals and open new accounts. I often wonder what the world would be like if successful Christian businessmen would set aside one day a week to pursue the Kingdom of God with the same level of gusto that they reserve for the paper chase.

When I was going through my worst times I didn't want a new job, or another side hustle, but even so I was constantly approached for opportunities that always involved someone asking me for money upfront. I've never been interested in paying to join an MLM or investing in a startup that hadn't quite started up yet. As it turns out, I'm not much of a joiner, I'd much rather partner with someone who's doing something new and amazing or blaze a trail with a few like-minded friends. The financial security that's offered by franchises doesn't really do much for me.

More importantly, I think the Western ideal of financial freedom (as it's practiced) usually leads to greed and bondage. Jesus wants the church to be a real family that sticks together through tribulations and hardship. The American dream sounds great in theory, but in reality, it leaves little room for orphans, widows, foreigners, prisoners, and people like myself. I'm done chasing the American Dream because my citizenship is in Heaven. That's why I wrote this book, and I hope it encourages you to reconsider your goals, and gives you a greater appreciation for fellowship and discipleship.

I've often heard today's youth described as the fatherless generation, and that's true both figuratively and literally. I hope my stories inspire you to do more for the next generation. Jesus came not to be served, but to serve, so let's follow His loving example. My prayer for you is this; if the plight of the lost and dying world has never robbed you of sleep, then I hope tonight will be the first time you stay up all night praying for strangers, acquaintances, Facebook friends, and people like me.

Chapter 3

Moving on

"So don't be afraid; you are worth more than many sparrows." -Matthew 10:31 NIV

"You will find what you are looking for when you realize God has placed those longings in your heart as a divine desire; your hunger is a gift from God to draw you to Him. It's a holy want with a holy fulfillment. Everything you really need and want is offered by and found in Him." -Mike Bickle

It took a long time for me to heal from the costly mistakes of those wilderness years. My spiritual recovery was not a straight line and that's OK. Preaches always remind us that God will forgive anything, but they usually forget to mention this fact; the excruciatingly painful, natural consequences of sin don't always vanish into thin air just because you said you're sorry. At times we must do our time and pay for our crimes before we learn our lessons.

That's right, God allows a certain level of tribulation and hardship because that's life. Also, it's important to realize that constantly bailing you out wouldn't be the fatherly thing to do. Jesus isn't a genie in a bottle, He's a real person with emotions. Once we grab a hold of that fact we can begin to understand the deeper truth of His great love.

When I was out of church I still prayed every day, but I was living in unrepentant sin. Even when I had a lot of money, that was not proof of God's approval, it was proof that the rain falls on the just and unjust alike. The Lord blessed me and He did protect me from the fallout of many dumb decisions, but I missed out on most of what He wanted to do through me during that season.

I was not walking by faith or keep my vessel filled with the oil of the Holy Spirit (Matthew 25:1-13). The first church I attended after my four hiatus was alright but it was too traditional and liturgical for me. It was a young, emergent hipster congregation that met in a beautiful, historic church building. The sermons were brilliant and the music was folksy and original.

The leaders didn't want anything to do with Evangelical alter calls or the controversial gifts of the Holy Spirit. This made me feel even more like an outsider. The people were friendly but a bit aloof from my perspective. The pastor didn't make a big deal about tithing or offerings. If you wanted to give, there were a couple of plain wooden boxes in the back.

The music was wonderful and the teachings were fascinating, but the pastor preferred the kind of intellectualism that never asked anyone to repent or change their ways. I never felt the slightest tinge of conviction and sin was rarely mentioned by name. I fell into a powerless theology that was overly philosophical and spiritually impotent. Deception blinded me from the severity of my sins.

After saving up some money, I moved to Los Angeles to pursue a career in music and joined a church called Mosaic. It's led by the brilliant author and speaker Erwin McManus. Their Sunday evening service was held in a rented secular venue (The Mayan) which was always packed full of creative artists, musicians, writers, and actors. It was far from perfect, but this was a significant improvement over my previous situation and I loved that place.

I continued to make little exceptions for my favorite sins which stunted my spiritual growth. I did alright in business at times, and I began writing regularly. By my late twenties a hope deferred made my heart sick because my music was floundering. I had endured a long string of difficulties at work and the stress of many bad decisions.

Even when I was flush with cash I didn't manage my money well. That merely enable me to experiment with designer drugs and indulge in expensive bad habits. I started spending more money on alcohol and cigars to cope with stress at work. I was a slave to various forms of lust, which eventually led to the idol I had conquered a decade earlier.

I was frustrated like the Israelites in Exodus who walked around in the wilderness for years without getting anywhere. I wasn't chasing pleasure because I was depressed, but all those depressants certainly left me feeling like garbage. It was a trap. When I think about my old ways, as a selfish, carnal person who simply drifted from one party to the next, a verse from Ezekiel comes to mind. This is how the

Lord feels when we play the Harlot with many lovers.

"I have been broken over their whoring heart that has departed from me and over their eyes that go whoring after their idols." -Ezekiel 6:9 ESV

Sin was robbing me blind. All those low-level pleasures were keeping me away from the great pleasure that comes only from pursuing God. I constantly wanted to feed my serotonin and dopamine receptors by smoking pot, and having sex. When I went to church I enjoyed the service but I felt like a spectator, always on the outside looking in. I wanted more but I was double minded, which left me dull and my heart was calloused.

Those choices led me to a string of unfruitful business ventures and a brief, failed marriage. My divorce was the last straw, and the feeling of despair and rejection hurt more than anything I've ever experienced. I never thought in a million years that I would end up divorced like my parents. I always told myself that I wouldn't end up like them, but this shattered those illusions. In reality, every one of my long term sexual relationships ended up like a divorce in God's eyes.

To be honest, this was more like my 4th or 5th divorce, not my first. Each time I lived with a girlfriend and then gave up it tore me up on the inside. Now I was completely devastated because the full impact of my life choices finally hit me. Instead of falling on the rock and being broken, it fell on me and I was crushed completely.

The emotional dam broke, but instead of repenting right away, I felt sorry for myself and became a screen junkie all over again. I let myself go and all that self pity and sorrow led to sins like pornography, gluttony, and sloth. I never used hard drugs or hooked up with a prostitute. I didn't go on a wild crime spree or commit some white collar crime, but the so called "small foxes" in my life were ruining my vineyard all over again.

I met Christians who would look me in the eye and say it's fine to live with your girlfriend or get drunk once in a while, but they weren't suffering for my sins or pulling me out of the pit when I needed help. The devil doesn't need a dramatic meltdown or a big scandal to keep you in bondage. All he needs to do is make you comfortable enough to embrace and accept whatever sins you're currently enjoying. Just start calling evil things good, and there's no telling how far you will fall.

All of these events happened right around the time that Netflix streaming was gaining popularity. I started binge watching movies and hanging out at a retro video store. I also took the liberty of downloading whatever I couldn't obtain through the proper channels. Some say that bootlegging movies is no big deal, but those websites featured tons of porn. They put it in my face when I wasn't looking for it, which made it extremely hard to break free from that once I dove into the deep end of the sewer.

Besides, there's so much violence, exploitation, and sexual content in ordinary movies that it desensitizes the viewer and dehumanizes the actors. If you don't think it's a problem then it only proves that Hollywood has successfully dulled your senses. Jesus can restore your soul, but you'll have to do your part. The Bible reminds us that we are surrounded by a great cloud of witnesses, and all of Heaven is rooting for us, so why would you want to waste your life in front of a TV?

"Behold, I am coming soon, bringing my recompense with me, to repay each one for what he has done. I am the Alpha and the Omega, the first and the last, the beginning and the end." Blessed are those who wash their robes, so that they may have the right to the tree of life and that they may enter the city by the gates. Outside are the dogs and sorcerers and the sexually immoral and murderers and idolaters, and everyone who loves and practices falsehood." -Revelation 22:12-15 ESV

In a matter of weeks my seemingly harmless hobby spiraled into a nasty habit. Smartphones and tablets suddenly allowed me to watch movies anywhere, and I've always loved having the latest electronics. Before long, my soul was sick from the heaviness and toxicity of sin. The wages of sin is death whether you believe it or not, and a steady diet of filth will never produce good fruit. God's clear call to holiness is a lifeboat.

The churches I went to were welcoming and friendly, but no one ever challenged me to repent or pursue holiness. Keeping the conversation polite was very important in most places. Life wasn't going as planned, so I turned to carnal pleasures and the fantasy world of cinema. Movies helped me forget about my worries for a while, but my divorce was so painful that I wanted to die. In a way, it was good that she dumped me. God used that situation to bring about His redemption.

Up to this point I was often the one who gave up easily when the going got tough in romantic relationships. After my ex left me, I immediately lost my taste for the party life. I had more money than I'd ever had before, but it did nothing to ease the pain. It was so traumatic that I threw away my weed and didn't even think about drinking for a long time. I had finally hit rock bottom.

Even so, the grief was so intense that I shut down emotionally and started binge-watched movies at home in bed all day. I must have laid around for a month before I decided to gird up my loins, face my problems, and seek help from a Christian counselor.

I cried out to the Lord and He answered my prayers. I repented for my sins and humbled myself before His throne of grace. As soon as I had a true change of heart (which means I stopped sinning) He broke through my mess and opened the floodgates of Heaven. Suddenly, I found an awesome Christian mentor but it was no coincidence. God's timing is perfect, I had to come to the end of myself and lay it all down at the foot of the cross. Over the course of the next two years I developed a friendship with a brilliant counselor who's still a good friend to this day.

To his credit, Roger Savill has never charged me for his services. His family invited me over for dinner and a weekly Bible study. That was the first time I attended a Bible study since High school and now I was thirty years old. It's hard to wrap my mind around all the blessings of that friendship that came as a direct result of repentance. I turned away from my sins, it wasn't just a matter of changing my mind or attitude.

I didn't go through any formal, American-styled therapy sessions or psychoanalysis. Most American counselors wouldn't dare treat me like a brother, and I think that may be part of the problem. Rodger and I mostly just sat around and talked about life. My healing came through a hundred hot meals, regular Bible studies, and fatherly advice.

Rodger is the real deal and I'm honored that he wrote the forward to this book. It's fitting because I could not have done this without his help. Rodger became the mentor I had always wanted. All I had to do was turn from my sins (and move halfway around the world to New Zealand). I was the one causing all the delays and blockage, not God. The Lord wanted this more than I wanted it for myself. The same is true in your life, God isn't holding back unless you're forcing His hand by covering yourself in sin. God is Holy and most Christians don't understand that or appreciate what it means.

Rodger met with me two or three times per week until I recovered from my worst wounds. His wisdom and guidance helped facilitate the healing process which led to an incredibly productive season of spiritual growth. He has a reputation for helping people who seem to be hopeless. I spent almost two years in New Zealand and it was a wonderful time.

Thanks to God I'm on the narrow path after years of wandering through the wilderness. Now I'm married with kids, and I stay fairly busy with work, ministry, and a growing family. It's hard to find time and energy for everything I want to pursue but at least now I'm headed in the right direction.

"You have planted much but harvest little. You eat but are not satisfied. You drink but are still thirsty. You put on clothes but cannot keep warm. Your wages disappear as though you were putting them in pockets filled with holes!" - Haggai 1:6 NLT

That verse perfectly describes the first ten years of my adult life. It's easy to become distracted and tempted, but when I obey the Lord and follow His lead, His joy flows through me in waves. The peace that I feel on a bad day is incredible. I'm more selective now when it comes to my free time. I'm older but my health is better than it was back then.

I rarely watch movies or TV, and it's easier to stay away from my old ways. We all stumble in many ways, but let's be clear, we do not all live in willful disobedience and a lifestyle of sin. I turn off the TV when it falls below my standards (which is often) and being selective makes it more fun when I find something worth watching.

When I moved back to America I met the most incredible woman who became my wife about a year later. Adjusting to married life was challenging after so many years of rebellion. As I've said before, God forgives us freely, but sometimes the wounds take time to heal. The good news is that His grace is sufficient and I've learned to lean on my Beloved Christ more and more.

My beautiful wife Melody is patient, kind, and even-tempered. Her love helps me in ways she'll never know and she holds me accountable without being overbearing. She is my best friend, a talented musician, artist, and science nerd. I know a lot of guys claim this but my wife is a Proverbs 31 woman.

When I was in Bible school I read a book about Keith Green called *No Compromise* which was written by his wife, Melody Green. It was an amazing book that impacted me so much that I prayed earnestly for God to help me find a woman like Melody, but what I actually said out loud was "God please send me a Melody" and He answered that prayer literally. God's love is more than practical, it's lavish, and extravagant.

Our two daughters are wonderful, they make me smile and laugh every day. Having kids helps me see life from a different point of view, and sometimes it makes me feel like a kid again. Having a family is a huge blessing and I'm excited to see what God has in store for our future.

Chapter 4

What is Idolatry?

"I am the LORD your God, who brought you out of the land of Egypt, out of the house of slavery. "You shall have no other gods before Me. "You shall not make for yourself an idol, or any likeness of what is in heaven above or on the earth beneath or in the water under the earth." -Exodus 20:2-4 NASB

i·dol·a·try

ī′dälətrē/
noun: idolatry; the worship of idols or a physical object as a representation of a god.
extreme admiration, love, or reverence for something or someone.
synonyms: idolization, fetishization, fetishism, idol worship, adulation, adoration, reverence, veneration, glorification, lionization, hero-worshiping "the prophets railed against idolatry"

What is idolatry? The definition at the top of this page can be found in a dictionary, but if you want to understand the harm that's caused by idol worship, you'll need to search the scriptures and seek the Lord. Idolatry was forbidden in the ten commandments, but if you want to know why God took such a strong stand against idols, then let's consider the lives of people who have ventured in both directions and compare their long term results.

This book is designed to be a case study on contemporary idolatry. It isn't exhaustive, but it has more than enough information for those who are serious about getting free and staying free. In short, when God says don't do something, that should be good enough, but the patterns of history show us that even God's generals have struggled with idolatry and played the harlot at times. (Jeremiah 3:1)

Idolatry is spiritual adultery and in God's eyes, that's equal to cheating on your spouse. If you've strayed from your faith, or given up on God, I hope this book will be part of your restoration and reconciliation. My inspiration for writing this came after my experience of working as a dog training. After that, I was encouraged to continue this study after a series of conversations with other Christians who were just as clueless as myself in regards to the dangers of idolatry.

Biblical literacy is at such a low rate that millions of

church-going believers cannot define words like worship, idolatry, or coveting. Knowing right from wrong is a baby step in our spiritual journey, if you fail to understand the basics, then you can't grow in maturity.

Why did I choose to make animals the primary focus of my study? Well, it's what I know. I write about them because I love animals. They mean a lot to me and this book comes from a place of affection, not condemnation. I can only draw from my life experience and what I've read or heard elsewhere. If you've walked with the Lord long enough, then you know He speaks through ordinary situations in our daily life. If I was into sports I would write from that perspective and use sports analogies to make the same points.

Jesus used farming and fishing parables to reach an ancient culture so that everyone could understand Him. Kings and peasants alike can understand what He was saying, and the same is true today. Teachers and preachers are wonderful, but when it comes to the basics, you don't need an expert theologian to reach up into Heaven and pull down a scientifically perfect interpretation for everything. (Romans 10:6,7)

Why did I name this book *Jobs, Dogs, and other Idols*? You can make an idol out of anything, but I feel that God put this on my heart a long time ago. The importance and timeliness of this issue hits me every time I meet Christians who freely admit that their dogs (or a career) is the center of their universe.

I don't have to pry, because most of the people I meet love to talk about themselves. It's amazing what happens when you're a good listener who allows the conversation to move beyond superficial topics like sports, food, and the weather. God provides incredible ministry opportunities when I'm patient enough to slow down and enjoy the journey.

I'm certainly not a qualified counselor, and I don't presume to take on that role. However, I love meeting people, and my work revolves around deep, meaningful conversations. There's no shortage of hurting humans who are eager to unburden themselves. I think that's the Wonderful Counselor working through me. That may be why I ended up working as a management consultant. It doesn't matter if I'm on an airplane, at a coffee shop, or walking along a nature trail. Sooner or later I find myself diving deep into a conversation about life.

The work of tearing down idols and enemy strongholds isn't just about worship, prayer, and intercession. Those are extremely important, but even the greatest prayer warrior cannot neglect the practical side, which is relational and communal.

Victory over idolatry is only possible when we learn to love our neighbor with grace and compassion for each other's weaknesses. I've never seen anyone break free from idolatry without the help of a few friends. Idolatry and the pride that keeps us isolated is often the root issue. It's the outward manifestation of selfishness, which is why the antithesis of idolatry is the choice to be selfless like Jesus.

In the first half of this book, we will explore idolatry as it relates to domestic animals. After that, we will cast a wider net and explore other common idols like work or even recreation. This book is not a condemnation of you or your pets. Instead, our goal is to "use sound judgment" (John 7:24, Proverbs 8:14) to understand our freedom in Christ, and the boundaries of right and wrong.

My goal is to be bold and speak the truth in love. It doesn't have to be one or the other. God is love, and that's true even with His warnings and woes; "The idols of the nations are silver and gold, the work of human hands. They have mouths, but do not speak; they have eyes, but do not see; they have ears, but do not hear, nor is there any breath in their mouths." - Psalm 135:15-17 ESV

A meaningful conversation about idolatry usually raises more questions than answers, but without a clear understanding of idolatry, how can you tell if it's a problem or not? It's impossible to avoid a pitfall that you aren't aware of, (it's called a blind spot for good reason) and walking closely with the Lord cannot happen apart from the pursuit of personal holiness. (Philippians 3:12)

I hope you are willing to take a long, hard look in the mirror, or as the Bible says "consider your ways". (Haggai 1:7) My prayer is that I can help you recognize idolatry before a benign molehill turns into a cancerous mountain. Without freedom from the strongholds of sin, you'll never grow into the kind of person who "is like a tree planted by streams of water, which yields its fruit in season and whose leaf does not wither— whatever they do prospers." -Psalm 1:3 NIV

I've never heard a Christian say idolatry is acceptable, but at the same time, I've rarely heard a pastor preach against idolatry. Almost anything can turn into an idol if we don't guard our hearts. (Proverbs 4:23) If walking with the Lord isn't your top priority, then you're not on the narrow road. Once you're on the broad road, something else will be your main thing, and it will pull you away from God's plan and purpose.

Idolatry is listed first and second among the ten commandments. In this case, first means foremost, and it's an indicator of preeminence and priority. Despite what you may have heard, Jesus never abolished the ten commandments when He did away with Old Covenant dietary laws, customs, and the oral laws of the Pharisees. God gave a New Covenant, but God does not change, and neither does His morality.

Idolatry manifests as an extreme devotion or veneration, and it can start with little statues, icons, portraits, or relics, but it always leads to the worship of those objects. Where's your treasure? If I asked your close friends or family members, what would they say you value the most? Is your identity wrapped up in your kids, sports, or a hobby? Is it all about money, or the pursuit of leisure?

God is jealous for you, (Exodus 20:5) and His desire is for you. Jesus wants to fill us with love for each other. It's easy to love an unseen God, but loving your neighbor is another story. Even so, love must rule your life. If you abide in him, his love is an easy yoke and a light burden. Idolatry is the heavy yoke of iron that we place upon ourselves.

When God has first place in our life, lesser priorities will naturally fall into their rightful place. Jesus wants to transform you into a joyful, peaceful temple, with a heart that's overflowing with love. As we cast away our bondage, walking with a clear conscience becomes the new normal. As we grow in intimacy with the Lord, the pull towards rebellion and adultery is easier to resist. Mature believers are those who come out of the wilderness, leaning on their beloved Christ. (Song of Solomon 8:5)

"All human relational problems—from marriage and family to friendship to neighbors to classmates to colleagues—all of them are rooted in various forms of idolatry, that is wanting things other than God in the wrong ways." -John Piper

When I was a boy, we always had a dog (or two), a few cats, the occasional bird and a big glass tank filled with colorful fish. I love dogs because they're excited when you come home and that feels great. Most dogs are friendly and eager to make new friends, and they're always ready for adventure. They have an unwavering loyalty and enthusiasm, which isn't true with most humans.

Dogs are all heart and it's hard to imagine life without their wagging tails and sloppy wet kisses. The Bible says we should greet each other with a Godly kiss (1 Peter 5:14, 2 Corinthians 13:12, Romans 16:16), but when was the last time you received a genuinely warm greeting? Even at church, most of us are a bit reserved. The best you can expect is a firm handshake or an awkward side hug.

Our culture has lost its moorings. The sexualization of media and entertainment has caused well intended people to overreact, and withdraw physically. At the same time, sexual deviance is at an all time high, so it's hard to blame anyone for feeling unsafe or insecure.

As it turns out, good old fashioned affection is extremely important and deeply meaningful. To be honest, there are times when I prefer the company of dogs over humans, can you blame me? That's why it's easy for me to sympathize with pet owners who take things a bit too far.

I've read plenty of articles that say adopting a dog reduces stress and leads to a longer life. No big surprise there. Without asking for much in return, they lavish their family with love and sympathy. I've rarely met a dog I didn't like, and the worst ones were always made that way by abusive humans. When a domestic animal becomes violent, or neurotic, it's almost always a human's fault. There may be an exception to that rule, but I haven't found it yet.

Dogs are hardworking and eager to please. They're a gift from God, who knew our needs and wants before we were born. At the dawn of creation, God appointed us as stewards over all creation. We must look after this incredible gift, but it would be wrong to value any gift more than the giver of all good things. (James 1:17)

No one will ever love you like Jesus, but at the same time, He will not share His preeminence with anyone or anything. The Lord of Heaven and Earth isn't your Lord unless you submit to His higher way. He is the King of my heart, but at the same time, He is the King of Kings. We like to see Jesus as our buddy, but most of us fail to understand the fact that He is God.

It wasn't a matter of God being selfish or picky, it's about Lordship. When the love of Christ becomes your highest priority, your love for humans will increase drastically. That's the gift of the Holy Spirit and your choice to follow his gentle leadership will lead to a radical lifestyle of generosity, grace, and selflessness. If you're sold-out for Jesus, you'll experience more than you could ever find through animals, a career, or hobbies.

Most of us never give 100% to the Lord, but I've seen tons of sinners give 100% for their favorite idol. Don't be lukewarm! Escapism and distraction isn't the solution to problems like depression or injustice. All the entertainment in the world can't cure a broken heart.

Jesus is the answer, He is the Great Physician who can heal anything. His love has never failed, and even when we give up, He is faithful. God is not a cold or distant deity. He is fully present, fully God and fully man. When He washed the feet of His disciples, He left no room for doubt about what we should do with our brief time on earth. We must serve one another and learn to love.

"If you love Me, you will keep My commandments... He who has My commandments and keeps them is the one who loves Me, and he who loves Me will be loved by My Father, and I will love him and will disclose Myself to him." -John 14:15,21 NASB

After the bills are paid each month, what takes the lions-share of your time and money? Do you invest heavily into video games, a fantasy football league, or your hair and makeup routine? How many hours do you spend every week on those items? It would be helpful to take a moment to do the math and count the cost. What about animals, how much time is devoted to your dogs each week? In the same way, if you spend more time "loving on" a sports car while only the scraps are left for your brothers and sisters in Christ, then you are neck-deep in idolatry.

If your PlayStation causes you to sin, tear it out and throw it away. For it is better that you lose a game than for your whole body to be thrown into hell. Don't be like the rich young ruler who walked away from Jesus disappointed, because of his wealth. You were set apart in your mother's womb for a holy purpose. So do everything within your power to "live a life worthy of the calling you have received." -Ephesians 4:1 NIV

Let's take a moment to consider the infamous young ruler from the Gospel of Mark (10:17-30, Luke 10:25-28 and Luke 18:18-30). This rich young ruler was smart enough to pursue an audience with Jesus, which was a brilliant decision. The Bible says he fell to his knees, which shows humility and sincerity. This enthusiastic young man was so close to the truth but walked away because he couldn't fathom the thought of abandoning his great wealth. His identity was found in money, not Christ.

I think most of us would give anything for a face to face encounter with Jesus, but the Gospels show us that people from all walks of life made the ultimate mistake of esteeming Him lightly. When we form unhealthy connections with anything; animals, objects, activities, etc., it grows into what's known as an enmeshment, which is a blurring of boundary lines. Jesus put it this way, "where your treasure is, there your heart will be also." -Matthew 6:21 NASB

Idol worship sets you up for a dysfunctional and drastically decreased development. It drags you down and slows your progress, like a swimmer trying to win a race while holding onto his comfort blanket. Idolatry is more than a crutch, it captures your heart and arrests your spiritual development.

In other words, your personal best is the bare minimum if you want to reign and rule with Christ in this age and the ages to come. Our life on earth is only temporary, I like to think of this life as a decades-long entrance exam that determines your eternal assignment. We won't just sit on a cloud in Heaven while playing a harp, it's going to be exciting and the last thing you want to do is throw away your treasures in heaven in exchange for a little pleasure today.

Beloved, you desperately need everything that God's

given you to pursue your highest purpose and calling. Misplaced passion and squandered gifts lead to a wasted life, but that doesn't have to be the end of your story. That's the broad road to destruction, but you can turn your life around right now.

Whether it's hard drugs, soft porn, or anything in between, you can be sure that every lane on the broad road to destruction leads to an engulfing, codependent relationship (in the short term), and after that, the second death. (Revelation 21:8)

If it would crush you to lose that certain something, then it might be an idol. If you can't live without it, then you might want to reconsider that relationship. True Christians have been bought at a price, and anything beyond faithfulness to Christ is harlotry.

"Jesus told his disciples, "If anyone would come after me, let him deny himself and take up his cross and follow me. For whoever would save his life will lose it, but whoever loses his life for my sake will find it. For what will it profit a man if he gains the whole world and forfeits his soul? Or what shall a man give in return for his soul? For the Son of Man is going to come with his angels in the glory of his Father, and then he will repay each person according to what he has done."
-Matthew 16:24-27 ESV

We might look down on someone who struggles with drugs or alcoholism, but most of us couldn't imagine life without video games or cable TV. Blindness is the rejection of God's objective truth. In some ways, the recovering drug addict is better off if he admits to being "wretched and miserable and poor and blind and naked" -Revelation 3:17 NASB

You might be able to recite hundreds of football stats or movie quotes, but when was the last time you memorized a Bible verse or shared the Gospel with a stranger? Jesus was right to rebuke the Pharisee by saying "the tax collectors and prostitutes will get into the kingdom of God before you." - Matthew 21:31 NASB

There are millions of Christians who say they follow Jesus, but from everything I've seen and read, only a small percentage of the western church is even attempting to live for Jesus. The average Joe puts far more gusto into his hobby, habit or career. Most of us are fanatical about work or play, but timid with outreach and evangelism.

Idolatry has driven the church into a powerless, polite stupor. Superficiality reigns supreme due to an unspoken understanding among the brethren. The silent majority has decided to tolerate their neighbor's sin because they don't want anyone holding them accountable. Just keep the conversation light and no one will be offended, right?

It's all good when life is going your way, but when disaster strikes, we need deeper and more meaningful Christian relationships. Time, money and energy are limited assets in your life. Therefore, if anything or anyone drives a wedge between you and God, it's an idol. If you can't say no to something, then you are a slave to that which holds your heart (1 Corinthians 6:12).

One hand washes the other and we must be willing to receive help because no one can be fully objective about themselves. Yesterday is gone, tomorrow is promised to no one, and today is all we have. Everyone will serve something or someone. My prayer is that this book will encourage you to run in such a way as to win the prize.

Chapter 5

Idol Worship

"You shall not make other gods besides Me;" -Exodus 20:23 NASB

worship (n.) Old English worðscip, wurðscip (Anglian), weorðscipe (West Saxon) "condition of being worthy, dignity, glory, distinction, honor, renown," from weorð "worthy" (see worth) + -scipe (see -ship). Sense of "reverence paid to a supernatural or divine being..." - Dictionary.com

"The Bible doesn't give a specific definition for worship. The English word, "worship," comes from two Old English words: weorth, which means "worth," and scipe or ship, which means something like "shape" or "quality." We can see the Old English word scipe or ship in modern words like friend ship and sportsman ship — that's the quality of being a friend, or the quality of being a good sport. So, worth-ship is the quality of having worth or being worthy. When we worship, we are saying that God has worth, that He is worthy. Worship means to declare worth, to attribute worth. We should declare that God is worthy, worth more than everything else put together. -kalaheomissionary.com

When asked about idolatry, the average person might think about the TV show *American Idol*, or a boy band from the '90s. If you ask a pastor, he may mention the golden calf in Exodus. Let's start here briefly to help us understand why it's so important. With God's help, Moses led the Hebrews out of Egypt, and I'm sure the massive Exodus was an incredible sight to behold.

Millions of former slaves tasted freedom for the first time as they walked out of Egypt with their families and an unknown number of Egyptians. At that moment, there was no doubt in anyone's mind about the power of God. There were no atheists in that area at that time. God performed earth-shattering miracles, and most were announced in advance. Pharaoh and his minions did everything they could with dark magic, but the devil himself couldn't keep up with the Almighty after a few rounds.

I can't imagine how the descendants of Abraham felt on that glorious day, after two hundred years of unbelievable oppression. With pillars of smoke and clouds of fire, God personally escorted a grand procession from bondage into liberty. This was the largest parade in human history, and it would have been visible for many miles. After a few weeks of walking toward the promised land, it's only reasonable to assume that life settled down a bit in the wilderness.

The supernatural became commonplace, which is hard to imagine. Water spouting from desert rocks and manna from Heaven couldn't satisfy the fickle crowds forever. I believe the story of Exodus was given, in part, to show us that love cannot be bought or commanded. God doesn't want mindless robots. Simply knowing that God is real does not guarantee that someone will love Him.

God is searching for the precious few who freely choose to love Him. He longs to share His home with real friends. Freedom was granted to the entire procession, but with freedom comes choices. After a few weeks of wandering in the wilderness, the massive crowds began to grumble and complain.   God has emotions and feelings just like us, and our lack of gratitude and loyalty deeply hurts His feelings. We aren't given all the dirty details about what happened to Israel in the wilderness, but we know a few bad apples began to spoil the whole barrel. Morale declined as everyone waited for Moses on Mount Sinai. Fear and doubt crept in and sin was crouching at the door.

Leaving the only home they'd ever known was uncomfortable, like a camping trip that just doesn't end. Why anyone would turn against the one true God who was manifest among the people, after only a few weeks is a real head-scratcher to me. Then again, the allure of rebellion is fairly straightforward. To put it plainly, we want what we want.

"Now faith is the assurance of things hoped for, the conviction of things not seen. For by it the men of old gained approval. By faith, we understand that the worlds were prepared by the word of God so that what is seen was not made out of things which are visible." -Hebrews 11:1-3 NASB

The Children of Israel didn't necessarily believe the calf was God. To them it most likely represented God. Perhaps this is what they thought God looked like, but this 'graven image' was beyond unflattering, it was blasphemous.

The image of a calf suggests they viewed the Lord as a source of provision and nothing else. In the natural, a calf represents material provisions and financial security. They were frequently worshipped in other ancient cultures. Cattle have always been a central part of agrarian life, especially before the advent of modern farming machinery.

Cows provide milk and meat, they plow fields and pull wagons. These beasts of burden make life easier on a farm. Dairy products are versatile, and tasty. Plus, the meat from one cow can feed hundreds. Back then, even a small field would have been significantly harder to work without a draft animal. That would be like trying to farm today without any kind of tractor or a truck.

The Hebrews suffered for centuries under the Egyptians, but as free men and women, it was necessary to have their faith tested. As the newness of miracles wore off, the reality of living in the wilderness set in. After a lifetime of clock-like predictability, they faced the fear of the unknown for the first time. Everyone was still recovering from extreme emotional trauma after generations of harsh, unrelenting, forced labor.

How does this relate to your life today? The Lord pulled you out of the bondage of sin and set you free. What will you do now that you're free? There might be a lot of wilderness between where you are right now and the fulfillment of your lifelong dreams. We want all the gifts God has to offer, but we're often reluctant to do our part while complaining about our circumstances.

We cry out for instant gratification, and when it doesn't come quickly, we doubt God's goodness and question His power. Even after decades of willful disobedience and self-inflicted bondage, we expect the Lord to fix everything instantly. The book of Exodus could have been written about a forty day journey. Instead, it was forty years, because of their extreme disobedience. The promised land was not physically far away, and the same is true for your destiny.

Israel should have arrived in a matter of weeks or months, as God intended, but forty days of mild inconveniences became forty years of bitter frustration. Every Christian goes through wilderness experiences in life. We've all had seasons of slowness and stillness that produce patience, and perseverance. Our progress depends on our attitude and the decisions we make.

Everyone is thrust into a war of attrition, whether they like it or not. That's a continual grinding down with hundreds of battles and challenges. Even gravity feels like it was designed to pull us down, but it can make us stronger.

The summer sun beats down on our back and the winter cold threatens our lives while causing our skin to crack, but that's life. We all face similar struggles, but the enemy wants you to feel like no one understands what you're facing. Don't buy the lie that says you're facing exceptional or unique temptations. That's a lie from the pit of hell. Everyone is fighting a difficult battle and you don't have to stay isolated.

"No temptation has overtaken you except what is common to mankind. And God is faithful; he will not let you be tempted beyond what you can bear. But when you are tempted, he will also provide a way out so that you can endure it." -1 Corinthians 10:13 NIV

This book was written to help you overcome idolatry and I hope you will help pull others out of the bondage that once held you down. That's what it means to be more than a conqueror. I pray that your life will never be the same after today. God will do his part, but you need willpower for the rest of the journey. Faith, obedience and long-suffering come first, understanding comes afterward.

God allows testing and trials for your strength and development. (Joel 2:25) He could easily remove every obstacle from your path, but that wouldn't help your level of maturity. You can't be an overcomer if you don't overcome adversity.

Rest is also important, especially if you tend to overwork, but most of what I see today is an overreaction to a works based theology that was more common in my grandparent's era. I've seen many preachers err a bit on many issues, but I've never witnessed an unabashed, works based theology from the pulpit. I have no idea what happens in your local church, and I'm sorry if you've had to suffer under a Pharisee pastor. All I can do is speak from my life experience and the testimony of others.

What's missing from sermons today? That all depends on who you're listening to, but if I had to put a fine point on it I'd say the pastors, priests, and ministers I've seen have mostly forgotten about the poor, orphans, widows, prisoners and foreigners. Others have forgotten about the Bible entirely, and preach good works as a path to Heaven. Overall, the fear of the Lord is absent from mainstream churches. We are living in the last days, "Laodicean" lukewarm era that goes on sinning so that grace may abound. (Romans 6:1)

We are His workmanship created to do "good work" and preach the Good News to the poor. If Jesus preached repentance, then you should too. Therefore, the next step in our spiritual journey is called working hard for the rest of our lives. How can anyone claim to love an unseen God while rejecting His call to love the people we see every day? (1 John 4:20) Jesus spoke about hell more than Heaven, and if you'll accept the good promises while rejecting the consequences of unbelief, that's called cognitive dissonance.

"In the field of psychology, cognitive dissonance is the experience of psychological stress that occurs when a person holds two or more contradictory beliefs, ideas, values, or participates in an action that goes against one of these three." -Wikipedia

"For since the creation of the world His invisible attributes, His eternal power and divine nature, have been clearly seen, being understood through what has been made, so that they are without excuse. For even though they knew God, they did not honor Him as God or give thanks, but they became futile in their speculations, and their foolish heart was darkened. Professing to be wise, they became fools, and exchanged the glory of the incorruptible God for an image in the form of corruptible man and of birds and four-footed animals and crawling creatures." -Romans 1:20-23 NASB

People say they trust the Bible, but they have all kinds of beliefs that contradict what Jesus said and did. Plenty of well educated pastors think they can essentially do one better than Jesus by preaching a message that's far sweeter than anything Jesus ever said. They ignore anything in the Bible that's unpopular in polite society. If that doesn't work they create an absurd new theology to explain it away.

The list of what's acceptable grows shorter every day, it won't be long before the worst ones give up the charade entirely. It's only logical to say that if you believed in Him, you would go out of your way to serve the Lord through charitable works and freely talk about the grace that saved you.

The finished work of the cross is the starting point for our race, not the finish line. The easy yoke and light burden of Jesus is wonderful, but that promise doesn't negate the physical burdens and toil of life in general.

In Matthew chapter 11, Jesus offered freedom from the heavy burdens of legalism, and the self-righteousness of the Pharisees. This isn't freedom from life's trails. The Lord is our healer and deliverer. His love lightens our mental and emotional burdens, but the Bible also admonishes us to "put on the helmet of salvation" (Ephesians 6:17).

That's an active instruction for you, not a passive, foregone conclusion. Jesus wasn't kidding when He said "be on your guard". (Matthew 10:17, Mark 13:9, Luke 12:15) Paul's letter to the Ephesians contains a valuable lesson on spiritual warfare because that's what we need. When the devil tries to get inside your head, you must fight back, it's not good enough to pretend like he doesn't exist. "Submit yourselves therefore to God. Resist the devil, and he will flee from you." -James 4:7 ESV

If this wasn't a real war, we wouldn't receive serious warnings from the Bible. If Jesus 'did it all' on the cross you would have received a trophy to admire instead of a Bible to study when you gave your life to Christ. Jesus paid it all, but

He won't do everything for you. Don't make an idol out of individual Bible verses, or inspirational quotes. Seek the full counsel of God, including the scriptures that are hard to digest and even harder to apply.

Willfully co-laboring with Christ is the only authentic response to salvation, because love is a verb. True love is a sacrificial lifestyle, it's not a warm, fuzzy feeling. If we don't love the humans in our life, then we couldn't possibly love God. Do you believe God is good? Do you believe that He has a good plan for your life? (Jeremiah 29:11) I pray that you will experience God's goodness a little more each day as you put your hand to the plow and never look back. (Luke 9:62)

Chapter 6

Steak for dogs & dog food for grandpa

"Today Christians spend more money on dog food than missions." - Leonard Ravenhill

"It is not right to take the children's bread and throw it to the dogs." -Matthew 15:26 ESV

Do you buy steak for your dogs? I'm not talking about scraps or leftovers, but choice cuts of meat specifically purchased for dogs. I've noticed a trend among wealthy pet owners who feed their dogs a diet of raw meat mixed with a few other ingredients. I understand that steak is closer to a carnivore's natural diet, and it's an improvement over cheap dog food, but dogs also behave like omnivores and scavengers. A true carnivore, like a lion, will starve before eating a carrot.

Dogs have successfully integrated with human households partially because of their willingness to eat almost anything. Raw meat is expensive, but do the health benefits justify the expense? In the poorest parts of the world, eating meat is an extremely rare treat. I'm not a vegetarian, but I would recommend sitting down with a vegan pet owner. Ask them how they keep their dogs healthy without meat.

You might be surprised at the variety of healthy, affordable choices. You probably shouldn't buy cheap kibble from the dollar store, but unless you work at a butcher's shop, there are plenty of options besides raw meat. It all goes back to the same questions; How much is too much, and where do you draw the line?

In my life, I'm unable to justify free-range, grass-fed, dog food for $5-10 a pound when there are hungry kids in my community. Before you object to my comparison, please hear me out. Readily available financial resources and manpower are available in a limited supply, and food shortages are always time sensitive situations. More importantly, Jesus made His feelings clear when He said "It is not right to take the children's bread and throw it to the dogs." -Matthew 15:26 ESV

Jesus coined this Proverbial phrase (or perhaps He recited it from common knowledge) when a Greek woman asked Him to heal her daughter. His response appears rude and dismissive at first glance, but it was said to test her faith. His statement assumes the fact about dogs to be self-evident. It's immoral to withhold resources from humans and cast it to dogs.

"To cast it to dogs.—The word used was diminutive in its

form, and as such pointed not to the wild, unclean beasts that haunt the streets of an Eastern city (Psalm 59:6), but to the tamer animals that were bred in the house, and kept as pets. The history of Tobias and his dog, in the Apocrypha, furnishes the one example in Biblical literature of this friendly relation between the dog and his master (Tobit 5:16). The answer has, even taking this into account, a somewhat harsh sound, but it did not go beyond the language with which the woman must have been familiar, and it was probably but a common proverb, like our "Charity begins at home," indicating the line of demarcation which gave a priority to the claims of the family of Israel to those of strangers." -Ellicott's Commentary for English Readers

Before we move on, let's remember the elderly fathers and mothers who are forced to eat dog food while someone's dog eats steak and eggs. A quick search online will yield as many gut-wrenching stories as you can stomach. If it hurts your heart to read stories about starving humans, please go to your local food bank or community shelter and sign up as a volunteer.

If you feel called to a youth ministry, that's great because most college kids can't afford steak either. If you have a heart for women specifically, offer to help at a battered women's shelter or a pregnancy crisis center. The majority of single mothers are living near (or below) the poverty line. Whether your rich, poor, or somewhere in between, we all need to be part of a local community of believers. So recruit a friend and go out together, "two by two" -Mark 6:7

Some of your neighbors are stuck in poverty, clinical depression and/or social isolation. You are the light of the world, a lamp on a stand, a city on a hill for all to see. Heaven is for real, so let's make the most of this short life. There's no shame in needing help, but it's often embarrassing to ask for help.

God hold's us accountable for the people we meet and the food we eat. You don't have to travel far to find open hearts or curious minds. The story of the rich man and Lazarus plays out every day, over and over again. (Luke 16:19-31) Real humans are searching for answers, and they would love to eat the scraps that fall from your table. Many are disadvantaged in ways you can only imagine. They're not just lazy bums or shiftless grifters. Even if they are making bad choices right now, God loves them and I hope you will intervene on their behalf.

What will you do in response to ongoing insults or tribulations? Will you hide from society and withhold support from anyone who reminds you of the ones who hurt you in the past? Or, you could respond with a "seven times seven" attitude towards forgiveness, with a conscience resolve to remain charitable with your words, time, money, and prayers. Would you be willing to show every paper receipt and online bank statements from the past year to the people in your Bible study group? How about the elders of your church?

Big-ticket items rarely break the bank, but the $5-$25 dollar range is another story altogether. Most of them will be pointless purchases that are easy to live without. For me those are usually impulses like fast food and entertainment. I've gotten better over the years, but the same is true for little time wasters. For you it might be ten minutes here and there for a video game or late night online shopping.

Your free time is important, but let's keep it free. Those precious restful moments are far more relaxing when they're free from soul-sucking addictions. We will cover this issue more in chapter 18, but for now, it's important to say that drugs, tobacco, and alcohol aren't the only vices that can be dangerously addictive. What's an easy solution? Jesus spoke about cutting off your hand if it's causing you to sin. "If your right hand makes you stumble, cut it off and throw it from you; for it is better for you to lose one of the parts of your body, than for your whole body to go into hell." - Matthew 5:20 NASB

Most of us take that figuratively, but there are plenty of pursuits that should be cut off for our benefit. At one point I had to "cut off" my home Internet service for a season. This was the easiest was to honor my true priorities. I'm glad I made this small sacrifice because the fruit of that decision was incredibly fruitful for my family. We could feel the level of intimacy rise in a matter of days.

Canceling your Wifi for six months may seem like a drastic step, but it helped me to create better daily routines and uphold a higher standard of personal integrity. Do you love God enough to cut off someone or something that's holding your back? Let's take one hour per day that's currently reserved for your favorite TV show. You could change the world with that extra chunk of time. It's hard to start new habits or retrain your mind with old habits. There are plenty of apps that track screen time and personal finances.

It only takes one hour a week to read through the Bible in a year, but most believers have never read the entire Bible. I think everyone should read the Bible daily, whether it's two pages or two hours. It's just as important as the water you drink. The Bible is food for your spirit, and you will be spiritually starved without the written word of God. When the word of God is delivered fresh to the renewed mind, it changes your perspective and sheds a new light on your priorities.

It's wonderful to see someone on fire for Jesus, and just like the passionate animal lover please remember you can't save everyone. Don't try to take every burden onto your shoulders, that's Gods job. Now you have the mind of Christ, you're well fed, and you're seated in Heavenly places. What's next? "Enter his gates with thanksgiving, and his courts with praise! Give thanks to him; bless his name! -Psalm 100:4 ESV

What we have in Jesus is more than enough. Each day you can wake up and quickly become fully prepared to make war against the doctrine of demons that says we should treat each other like savage animals. Darwin called it natural selection and his followers call it survival of the fittest. When someone applies this philosophy to humans it becomes that which "exalts itself against the knowledge of God." -2 Corinthians 10:5 NKJV

Cain asked God "am I my brother's keeper?" and the correct answer was yes. Will you be your brother's keeper? Jesus said feed my sheep, but the coward says 'every man for himself.' Survival of the fittest is cruel, animalistic and inhumane. Jesus said the poor will always be among us. (John 12:8) That's true, but that quote is often abused by immature believers who want to avoid being a good Samaritan.

When you hear an empty excuse like that, remember this; the devil also used the Bible against Jesus. (Matthew 4:1-11) So be careful to avoid taking a single line out of context. The Bible is crystal clear about how we should treat one another. There will never be a shortage of poor people, but you can help one person today and let tomorrow worry about itself. When humans deny their God given conscience, and adopt the standards of beasts, it always leads to an anti-Christ spirit. It's no wonder the book of Revelation reveals so much about the Beast.

Let your light shine, small as it may be, and God will bring the increase because He is always faithful. One act of kindness for today can be something as small as picking up the phone to call a lonely neighbor. You are the hands and feet of Christ, so buy a pizza and share it with a group of teenagers. Take the money you've saved up for idols "use worldly wealth to gain friends for yourselves, so that when it is gone, you will be welcomed into eternal dwellings." -Luke 16:9 NIV

Buy a new pair of shoes for the poor kids at church.

Invite an elderly widow over for a cup of tea. This is the easy yoke and light burden of Christ that leads to repentance and salvation. Your neighborhood is ripe for the picking. Are you too busy for God's will? Your actions alone will answer this question. You can stop the trend of pointless suffering for a few people with your discipleship.

God assigns everyone an ongoing mission to those within a few city blocks, (or a few country miles) of our home. You may have to travel further if you live in a suburban sprawl that's far from poverty. When I read stories about impoverished senior citizens who've been reduced to eating canned dog food, I wonder, how could we fail so badly? We have so many gifted teachers, books, videos, music, and conferences; more equipping resources than all of human history combined.

"How can you be so dead, when you've been so well fed?" - Keith Green

It's heartbreaking to know this is happening all over the world. I realize that some elderly people alienate everyone in sight, even their family, with anger and bitterness. If you can't talk to someone in your own family, please set aside time to connect with someone else in need. The church is your family, but most of us don't walk in that reality. It's going to be difficult at times, you can't force old people to be polite anymore than you can force a college student to volunteer at a retirement community.

Don't worry about what could go wrong, seek out a few people who are open to discipleship and bridge the gap. It's our job to break down generational barriers. It's not always pleasant, but it's worth the struggle because no one is beyond hope. Invite someone over for dinner and call a few neighbors each week to see how everything's going. "The poor man is hated even by his neighbor, but many are those who love the rich." -Proverbs 14:20 BSB

I know you have problems, we all have those, but God gives seed to the sower, not the talker. You might feel like you're drowning in a huge pile of debt, but if we're honest, one or two extra guests at the dinner table will not break the bank. Idols break the bank, not generosity. No one ever went broke by hosting a Bible study or a pot luck dinner. If money is tight, call the cable company and cancel your overpriced TV bundle.

Miraculous power and spiritual gifts are exciting and necessary. We should eagerly desire those, (1 Corinthians 14:1) but for now, I hope you will do whatever it takes to restore the spiritual gift of hospitality at home. What if you kept your used cars a few years longer? What if Jesus called you to buy a smaller home in a less desirable neighborhood? King Solomon put it this way, "Catch the foxes for us, The little foxes that are ruining the vineyards" -Song of Solomon 2:15 NASB

Little foxes are a metaphor for minor indulgences, teeny-tiny sins, and little white lies that we view as harmless. That's the devil's trick, to help you make excuses for anything small enough that it passes through your internal filter without any second thoughts. In our hearts we say, this is acceptable. Instead, let's ask, is this purchase (or time commitment) in line with my highest purpose and calling? Don't judge by size. Instead, consider the fruit it produces.

Suffering for the sake of bad decisions is not the same thing as suffering for the sake of the Gospel. Drowning in consumer debt from credit cards and new car loans doesn't make you a martyr, it's more like suicide. Find an accountability partner who will help you get better at saying no to the "small foxes" that destroy the potential of your spiritual vineyard. Jesus said, "I am the vine, you are the branches; he who abides in Me and I in him, he bears much fruit, for apart from Me you can do nothing." -John 15:5 NASB

Idolatry is the pesticide that poisons your connection

with Jesus and the body of Christ. I've heard so many people say they will do great things someday if they win the lotto or land a dream job, but planning to be generous in the future is insincere at best. Waiting for everything to line up before you jump into the fray is only an appropriate life goal for a preteen in middle-school. Don't eat the seed (time and money) that you have been given. Invest those seeds if you want to see a return.

When I was a child I thought like a child and reasoned like a child, but I regularly hear shockingly immature statements from middle aged adults in their prime. Do you honestly think God needs you to have a big pile of cash before being activated into a ministry? God isn't short on cash, but He did say the workers were few. The all too common wait and see mindset comes from a lack of faith and a misunderstanding of sowing and reaping. "But prove yourselves doers of the word, and not merely hearers who delude themselves." -James 1:22 NASB

There are no treasures or crowns of glory laid up in Heaven for good intentions. All we have is today, so let's take action now and work towards a better tomorrow. Each of us has an unlimited number of options in life. Even if you're a prisoner or a homeless beggar, you still have choices and will be judged by what you do with what's at your disposal. In the meantime, why would God promote anyone to a greater level of responsibility if they aren't faithful with what they've been given?

God doesn't need you to be rich to do great things. It's better to reconsider our definition of greatness. I love to read old, out of print Christian books. I've noticed that most were written about people who were poor or very near poverty for decades at a time. Those mighty men and women from history lived extraordinary lives with legendary faith. Their hope in Christ was not hindered by a lack of wealth.

Throw an extra slab of meat on the grill and fill up the

Croc-Pot, it's not hard. Buy a large bag of dollar burgers if you're can't cook. Most of us are generous with coworkers and clients, but they can easily repay you. (Luke 6:33-35, Luke 14:14) Take a step of faith and bless the immigrants who happen to be in your sphere of influence. Hospitality doesn't have to be formal like a Thanksgiving dinner, so feel free to keep it casual.

If you lack the courage to open up your home, that's OK. Start slow and God will stretch your faith little by little. Sometimes generosity must be served with a side order of risk. If you're concerned about safety, ask your friends and church family for help. Get together with your life group and make sack lunches. Take them to a local skate park or a late night outreach downtown when the pubs and clubs are active. Share the Gospel in these brief moments and always prepare your heart in advance with prayer, fasting, and worship.

Fair warning; you might need to give an hour of listening before you earn the chance to share five minutes of testimony. If you prefer something more organized, it's easy to find nonprofits and para-church organizations that need reliable volunteers. Some churches do a great job with community outreach. Others are more inwardly focused but it's best if we can learn to master intercessory prayer without ignoring evangelism.

If your church isn't directly helping the poor in your community, then schedule a meeting with your pastor and discuss your concerns. Then offer your services and be the change you want to see in the church. Do it as if you were serving Jesus Himself and not people (Ephesians 6:7). Choose to serve with the same level of passion that goes into your favorite hobby. If you're thinking about something specific right now, maybe God has put that on your heart for this season.

Chapter 7

Emotional support

"45% of pet owners say they like to spoil their pets, while more than a third say their pet understands their feelings better than most humans." - Mintel Pet Supplies

"The LORD God said, "It is not good for the man to be alone. I will make a helper suitable for him..." So the man gave names to all the livestock, the birds in the sky and all the wild animals. But for Adam no suitable helper was found." -Genesis 2:18,20 NIV

Should you rely on animals for emotional support? It's important to be respectful about this issue because it's deeply personal. First of all, if humans honored each other with mutual love and respect, we wouldn't need emotional therapy. Animals never judge, discriminate, or question your motives. Dogs don't hesitate to shower you with affection, and that's a gift from God. I've said it before and I'll say it again, I love animals.

Dogs have enriched the lives of many and well-behaved dogs can provide therapeutic benefits. Even so, we should all be concerned about the overall lack of quality research on therapy animals. At this point someone may accuse me of splitting hairs, but I don't see it that way. If there is any amount of willful rebellion against Christ in your life, it's too much. Jesus wants to heal you more than you want to be healed and only He can guide you back onto the narrow path. Perfection is a worthy pursuit regardless of our flaws.

When it comes to touchy subjects, one should ask, is this a hill worth dying on? For some the answer is a resounding yes, but it's hard to think of any issue that isn't hotly contested these days. Growing irreconcilability is a clear sign of the times. (2 Timothy ch 3)

Before we discuss emotional support animals, my first concern is how quickly the subject has become off-limits. That's the devil's strategy, to keep you isolated in silence. It's the same way every important topic. For example, if the enemy convinces you to avoid discussing personal finances, even among trusted friends, then you'll suffer as a direct result. When your bills are overwhelming and you feel hopeless, an attitude that says "this area is off-limits" is the same bad attitude that will lead you further into the pit of despair.

After all, what would your friends think? Your parents might not talk about money or emotions, but that's their problem. Stifling emotions and hiding your struggle can only make matter worse. Whenever you insist upon walking alone, you become easier to defeat. If you're stuck in an emotional, spiritual, or mental prison right now, Christ alone can set you free.

Enter the emotional support animal. The experts loudly demand that you don't call them pets. They claim the authority to redefine words, which is a dishonest tactic designed to frame conversations in a way that makes it easier to persuade without compelling evidence. Don't be fooled by the industry's efforts to redefine words, that's just marketing and manipulation.

I have a hard time with this subject. As a dog trainer I've met more than a few customers who freely admit that they dress their dogs in official-looking vests with patches just to skirt the rules at restaurants, hotels and other places. They laugh about it as if it were a big joke. To some, it's just too easy to get away with (what is in their eyes) a harmless little scam.

To clarify, this chapter isn't about service dogs. Professionally trained dogs are indispensable, hard-working animals that perform important tasks for the military, police, search and rescue, etc... Service dogs are almost always well behaved, and they make life better for physically disabled persons. Legitimate service animals are as rare as they are expensive. I think it's wrong to pretend like every animal is equal to a service animal just because they provide companionship or makes us feel better.

Emotional support animals can be wonderful, but my primary concern is the potential for abuse. Any long term dependency can hinder the process of recovery. We must consider the fruit, and resist the urge to rely on feelings. This new emotional support category began with great intentions but the good has been almost entirely overshadowed by opportunists who've turned it into a catchall excuse to skirt the rules in public places.

What does the research reveal? A quick search online (https://scholar.google.com/) provides scant research with mixed results on the issue of therapy animals. (1) (2) Based on everything I've read I'm sticking with my mother's advice when she sent me off to college. She said, "Don't buy an animal until you're financially stable and ready for all the extra responsibility." In many cases, the burden of caring for an animal will make a bad situation much worse. (3) (4) Here is an exert;

"A recent literature review by Molly Crossman, a Yale University doctoral candidate... cited a "murky body of evidence" that sometimes has shown positive short-term effects, often found no effect and occasionally identified higher rates of distress. Overall, Crossman wrote, animals seem to be helpful in a "small-to-medium" way, but it's unclear whether the critters deserve the credit or something else is at play." -Karin Brulliard

I think we're all guilty of conflating causation and correlation at times. We see something we like, and then we rush ahead without enough due diligence. We cling to experts who agree with our opinions while ignoring anything that doesn't reinforce our preferred conclusions. In many cases the responsibility of pet ownership is overwhelming and detrimental to their health. (5)

When considering the pros and cons of this subject, it's important to remember that Christians are called to a higher standard, even when we're treated badly. We must "Do nothing from selfish ambition or conceit, but in humility count others more significant than yourselves." -Philippians 2:3

For example; if a business owner doesn't want dogs inside her store, a mature Christian would gladly honor their request. That's a perfect example of "valuing others above yourself." Emotional support animals are still a relatively new concept. Well behaved animals are delightful, (unless you're afraid of dogs) but here's my main question: Do you feel compelled to bring your dog along everywhere?

It's fair to ask, how did our forefathers survive without a wide variety of creature comforts? Some will say, "they survived very badly" but I disagree. Comments like this reflect an ignorant, arrogant, false point of view. Discomfort has a purpose, and numbing the pain isn't always God's perfect solution. The painful symptoms that we manifest emotionally are allowed to help you find a solution, not an escape. Working out the real problem is the job of every overcomer.

I think we all tend to behave like selfish tyrants with our personal preferences, and that bad attitude needs to be crucified with Christ. Charles Spurgeon once said, "Be assured, there is nothing new in theology except that which is false." I think that applies to our present situation. When any pastor or priest tries to present a "new normal" that minimizes a challenging part of the Bible or places a demand on everyone else, it's only reasonable to treat that new idea with a healthy dose of suspicion.

The burden of proof belongs to those who wish to force their will onto others. In the name of tolerance, some of us are quick to jump every time a new theory is presented as a fact. We often chase new trends based on their popularity without stopping to consider whether or not it lines up with the scriptures. It's easy to get excited about new ideas, but we've largely failed to master the basic principals that Jesus and Paul taught in the New Testament.

From the perspective of my grandparent's generation, we've become overly soft and permissive. An endless stream of modern conveniences and luxuries leave us blind. As a middle-class American in the twenty-first century, I am living on the cutting edge of comfort. Anyone with a lifestyle similar to me is an outlier compared to everyone in history.

America is called by God to be the world's biggest exporter of Christian Charity, and in some ways we are generous. Unfortunately, those efforts are greatly diminished by our unquenchable appetite for consumables. We are unrivaled as importers of drugs, (both legal and illegal) pornography, and cheap, plastic, disposable junk from around the world. Christians in China are now sending missionaries to America because many of our churches have lost their zeal.

The strength and perseverance of previous generations has been rejected and forgotten. Instead of learning from history, we compare ourselves to ourselves (within our close-knit social circles) and fail to see how far we've fallen. Paul put it this way; "Not that we dare to classify or compare ourselves with some of those who are commending themselves. But when they measure themselves by one another and compare themselves with one another, they are without understanding." -2 Corinthians 10:12 ESV

Westerners pridefully pat themselves on the back for the technological breakthroughs of our peers without realizing what we've lost morally. Our politically correct culture scorns the legacy of the pioneers who worked backbreaking jobs and paved the way for our future. You probably don't have to wash your clothes by hand, or chop firewood and haul buckets of water before you cook or bathe in the morning.

Now, the younger generations demand all sorts of special accommodations to feel comfortable within the most comfortable society that has ever existed. God loves to comfort the afflicted, but at times, He afflicts the comfortable to spur us on toward love and good works. (Hebrews 10:24) Comfort isn't the solution to every problem. Pain and discomfort can be excellent teachers, but not when we constantly numb the pain. Momentary relief can be found through distractions, pleasure, drugs, etc., but too much self-medication makes everything worse in the long run. Don't make an idol out of comfort.

Instead, seek the Lord in solitude, and make room for the Holy Spirit to work through humans who were created in the image of God. We are the church, we are the body of Christ, we have the mind of Christ, we are seated in heavenly places. Your fellow believers are here to help pull you out of despair. These are your neighbors, pastors, elders, etc.

The only downside is human nature. It can be very harsh and judgmental. It's important to be gracious and forgiving. The pursuit of unity is inseparable from the second greatest commandment, to love thy neighbor. Humans have hurt you, rejected you, and deeply offended you, but if you want God's forgiveness, there's a condition, to always forgive every human.

We can love our neighbors only as much as we learn to lean on our beloved Lord. (Song of Solomon 8:5) Jesus is the only crutch that leads to eternal life and the healing you need today. Depending on the Lord is the only dependency that will not fail. Every other temporary fix will fall short. The fear of the Lord is a reliance upon the Lord. If you truly fear the Lord, you will never fear another man again, and as you learnt to depend on the Lord you won't worry about the future.

Where should we draw the line between nature and nurture? We have freedom in Christ, so you'll have to judge for yourself. Only God can see what you do when you're alone. What I can say for sure is this; words fail to describe how much love and affection the Lord has in store for those who are sold out for Jesus. (Galatians 2:20) No one is perfect, but this is an all or nothing proposition. Who among us can honestly say God has let us down?

The book of Genesis explains our responsibility to lovingly care for all of creation. Affectionate animals are a gift from God, but that doesn't mean pet ownership is an answer to your problems. Believers must press in for a breakthrough. Seek healing and deliverance, even if it takes years or decades. Start where you are, and don't be afraid to get creative, but the goal is to arrive at a place where you can socialize in public without a therapy animal.

"God blessed them; and God said to them, "Be fruitful and multiply, and fill the earth, and subdue it; and rule over the fish of the sea and over the birds of the sky and over every living thing that moves on the earth."" -Genesis 1:28 NASB

"A surprising number of diseases can be spread from animals to humans and vice versa. They're quite common in fact, and it's estimated that more than 6 out of 10 infectious diseases in humans originated in animals. Zoonotic disease may be spread from family pets, petting zoos, fairs or encounters with wildlife." -Dr. Karen Becker

Do you know what every superhero has in common? Whether we're talking about Superman, the Avengers, the Xmen or any comic book hero, they're all alike in two respects. First of all, they're make-believe. Secondly, their superpowers are almost always destructive.

They might have other skills, like the ability to read minds or heal quickly, but it's always in the context of killing bad guys to save the world. Jesus died to save mankind from a real devil and a real hell. It may sound cheesy to say this but Jesus Christ is the only real superhero and He wants to fill your life with the power of the Holy Spirit. Yes, the same power that conquered the grave. The story of our savior isn't fiction.

Jesus is fully God, and fully man. He was born of a virgin, He performed many miracles and healed the sick. Jesus never sinned, but He died for our sins, rose from the dead and is now seated on a throne in Heaven. Jesus said we would do even greater things. His creative power is available to faithful servants who walk with Him. Jesus didn't call us to be killers who avenge. When we crave revenge, He says "vengeance is mine, I will repay". King Jesus teaches us to forgive, to turn the other cheek, and to love our enemies.

The same power that conquered the grave lives in me. The power of the cross is available for Christians to perform signs, wonders, and miracles. We speak healing into existence by faith. I've been a first hand witness to everything from financial miracles to physical healings. We have the power to organize, unify, and speak prophetic words that encourage, inspire, and give hope to the hopeless.

Society is obsessed with superhero movies and Star Wars characters, but Jesus wields the greatest power in existence. We are called to be peacemakers and reconcilers. Even when the devil rages and the end times usher in a flood of war, famine, plagues, and persecution The power of the cross will continue to eclipse all the chaos and restore hope to a lost and dying world.

The power of the Holy Spirit will continue to protect and direct the church as we march forth to victory. The great falling away will be overpowered by the Great Awakening, and creative miracles will increase and abound during the last great revival. This mighty movement of powerful champions will continually rack up victories until the very moment that Jesus returns in Glory on a white horse.

If you don't believe in miracles, that's called unbelief. According to your faith, so shall it be. Millions of nominal believers (cultural Christians) refuse to walk by faith. They still face all kinds of hardship and aren't immune from striving, but they can never enter into God's true Sabbath rest without turning to God with sincere repentance and a willingness to join the great harvest. Your words and actions have immense power, it's time to stand up and do something that will last forever.

"Death and life are in the power of the tongue, and those who love it will eat its fruits" -Proverbs 18:21 ESV

The NLT says "The tongue can bring death or life; those who love to talk will reap the consequences." What will you do if the doctor gives you a discouraging diagnosis? The choice is yours. Does every Christian receive healing every single time they pray? No, but whatever you do, don't give up hope.

Will you speak words of encouragement, and make better life choices, or will you give full vent to your anger and verbally vomit on everyone in your path? The final judgment at the end of this age isn't centered around what's happened to you. It's all about how you response to the mixed bag of difficulties that we all face. "Do not give what is holy to dogs, and do not throw your pearls before swine, or they will trample them under their feet, and turn and tear you to pieces." -Matthew 7:6 NASB

What does this have to do with idolatry or emotional support animals? If you've been to an airport recently you've probably noticed an influx of adults traveling with emotional support animals. All opinions aside, dogs are incredibly useful for therapy with conditions like PTSD. I would love to see an increase of volunteers with well-behaved dogs at places like Children's hospitals and retirement communities.

In all my research about therapy animals, I've barely seen a shred of consideration for humans who suffer from animal allergies. Those can be excruciatingly painful and debilitating. There is also little consideration given to the rights of employers, business owners, and landlords. True love isn't rude, inconsiderate or forceful. Love never demands the right to damage or forcefully control someone else's property. That isn't loving, it's tyranny.

I recently read about someone who tried to take an "emotional support" peacock onto her flight. Another article featured an emotional support pit-bull that attacked two Delta employees. Yet another article told about a woman who tried and failed to escort her emotional support hamster onto a commercial airplane. After her beloved rodent was denied passage, she simply flushed it down the toilet. Crazy situations like these are the natural result of unrestrained carnality.

Incidents like those (and many others) have forced airlines to publish a long list of banned animals including; turkeys, ferrets, snakes, hedgehogs, and any animals with tusks or hooves. As Adam Ford of the Babylon Bee famously quipped, "the Woke Monster of political correctness can never be satisfied. The more you feed it, the more it demands."

Christians need to wake up, stand up, and unite against anything that attacks freedom and love. The church is sending mixed signals because Christ is not the head of every so-called Christian church. True unity can only happen when we unite around the inerrant word of God. What shall we do? Here's a good starting point; "We destroy arguments and every lofty opinion raised against the knowledge of God, and take every thought captive to obey Christ..." -2 Corinthians

10:5 ESV

Every human tries to fill the God-shaped hole in their heart with work, pleasure, or recreation, but the heart needs more than retail therapy or animal companionship. God is faithful, He will set you free when you repent and stop living in willful disobedience. It's hard to hear clearly when you fail to obey God's Word and your God-given conscience.

I've heard too many good reports to doubt God. Your miracle could happen instantly, or it may take years, but until then, hold on the hem of His cloak. (Matthew 14:36) That's a metaphor for faith, and I've personally experienced His healing touch many times. Let's learn from the parable of the persistent widow who kept petitioning the unjust judge. (Luke 18:1-8) She didn't quit, and neither should you. Don't stop knocking until your prayers are answered.

"For a time is coming when people will no longer listen to sound and wholesome teaching. They will follow their own desires and will look for teachers who will tell them whatever their itching ears want to hear." -2 Timothy 4:3 NLT

"Humans alone have eternal souls, which confers a unique moral status... But the animal-rights cause is quite different: Instead of elevating human rights, this cause diminishes them by insisting we eliminate the distinction between humans and animals. It would be our moral undoing." -Charles Colson

The world says "nothing's too good for my baby" and that's quickly turned into an attitude that says "nothing's too good for my doggy." Perhaps the most startling trend I've noticed recently is a passive acceptance of dogs in church on Sunday. This is yet another brand new normal that some are eager to fight over. I've visited hundreds of churches in various cities, states, and nations without seeing a dog inside of a church until recently. Then, all of a sudden, the floodgates opened.

Now I see dogs in church regularly, as if it had always been this way. Some will call this an outdated tradition that needs to change. If this is just a tradition, what's wrong with that? I think it's a sign of the end times. Beloved, there are plenty of places where dogs are welcome. I'm suggesting we make one place so special that it's treated differently from every other place. For example, I like to dress up for church and I do it to honor God.

At the same time, I appreciate casual churches because dressing up has become a stumbling block to those who cannot afford dress clothes. House churches and home groups are great because you can do as you please in the privacy of your home as long as it honors the Lord. I think most of this conforms with "The Law of Liberty" from Romans ch 14.

We must accept those with weak faith, so please don't put words in my mouth. The church building is God's house, and your church was built, dedicated and set apart for the sole purpose of ministry. This was done with a solemn, sacred vow. What I'm suggesting isn't legalism, it's integrity, reverence, and honor.

I was fortunate to grow up in a house with thousands and thousands of dusty, old Christian books from a wide range of publishers. In all my reading, both at home and elsewhere, I've never seen anything that could legitimize having dogs in church. Saint Francis is the most common historic figure whose name is routinely invoked for the sake of convenience. People will search high and low for exceptions to the rule and craft their doctrine around anomalies. Francis of Assisi was a friar, deacon, and preacher with a wonderful reputation that's been hijacked by animal lovers.

His legacy and fame is misused by idolators who seek to legitimize the worship of animals and nature. On social media, Francis has become the patron saint of naturalists, shy, confused Christians, and atheists who wrongly quoted as saying, "Preach the Gospel at all times. Use words if necessary."

That quote sounds nice if you've never read the Bible. However, if you study the Bible, then you already know it directly contradicts a clear, central themes of the New Testament. (Mark 16:15, 2 Timothy 4:2, etc.) Every disciple of Christ is directly commanded to spread the Gospel through the word of their testimony in the Great Commission.

Francis certainly loved and cared for God's creation, I wish we all did the same, but he never said anything anything of the sort. Much has been written about him so it's easy to fact check. The Apostle Paul must have run across the same nonsensical passivity when he said "how shall they hear without a preacher?" -Romans 10:14 KJV

Aspiring bloggers and motivational speakers are always eager to coin a phrase that's both spiritual and original, but if it directly contradicts the Bible, it should not be shared. Here's a better quote that aligns more closely with the Bible, "Practice what you preach." Don't be a hypocrite, but don't be a silent coward either.

Actions speak louder than words, but words are required if you're not ashamed of the Gospel. You can't preach without words, and you don't have to be perfect before you start telling the world about our perfect savior. Believe it or not, preaching is part of everyone's mission, even if you're an introvert. You don't have to be an outgoing evangelist to to share your testimony or offer wise council. Preaching might not be your primary gift or vocation but it's an important part time gig. The harvest is plentiful, and ripe for the picking, but bold preachers are few and far between.

You don't have to preach a formal sermon in a pulpit, just be yourself. It can done in a small group or with an audience of one. The enemy wants you to remain silent, but don't take his advice. When someone quotes that well intended line about using words if necessary, it's usually due to confusion, political correctness, or an aversion to preaching. Forgive them Lord, they know not what they do.

When someone posts a quote like that, what they mean to say is, "why don't you keep your mouth shut and go do some charity work?" It's not an entirely unfair criticism. The church has too many arm chair experts and keyboard warriors who don't feel led to personally participate in the work that Jesus commissioned us to do.

As for Saint Francis, he followed Christ, and some say he preached to animals. If that's true, he was only guilty of a little youthful exuberance. I wish more of us would get so excited about Jesus that we practiced our preaching in front of the family dog. Francis of Assisi was far from perfect, but he was well aware that Jesus didn't die for your poodle's sins. Praying for your pets is fine within reason, but worshipping animals is idolatry and the idolator has no place in Heaven. (citation Revelation)

"What agreement has the temple of God with idols? For we are the temple of the living God; as God said, "I will make my dwelling among them and walk among them, and I will be their God, and they shall be my people. Therefore go out from their midst, and be separate from them, says the Lord, and touch no unclean thing;" -2 Corinthians 6:16-18 ESV

"And touch not the unclean thing - In Isaiah, "touch no unclean thing;" that is, they were to be pure, and to have no connection with idolatry in any of its forms. So Christians were to avoid all unholy contact with a vain and polluted world. The sense is, "Have no close connection with an idolater, or an unholy person. Be pure; and feel that you belong to a community that is under its own laws, and that is to be distinguished in moral purity from all the rest of the world." -Barnes Notes on the Bible

I think most Christians would agree that dogs should stay home on Sunday, but they're afraid of saying anything.

They don't want to be viewed as rude or unwelcoming. Blind guides say it's OK and then chastise me for having a traditional point of view. In the name of political correctness, we turn a blind eye, but even if a blind person brings dog to church, the sanctuary must remain sacred.

How can we do that without offending a disabled person? I said earlier that service animals are the exception to the rule, but we can still offer special accommodations. Churches can easily prepare a place for dogs to rest comfortably outside, in the shade, or in a separate building. Then, Volunteers can accompany disabled people as necessary. It's not hard to honor everyone with special needs and make them feel welcome.

From my experience, people who suffer from the worst disabilities are not easily offended. They're tougher than most of us and rarely suffer from the kind of first world problems that drive others to want an emotional support animal. Unless you need a service animal, bringing a dog into church shows a lack of reverence and respect. I think every church should post a No Dogs sign on the front door if it becomes a problem.

Does it offend you when I say dogs are unclean animals? I'm not talking about Old Testament laws or the oral traditions of Pharisees. Neither was Paul in 2 Corinthians ch 6. Unclean in this context means dirty, dogs can be very gross at times, and it's OK to state the truth plainly. Have you ever hear the popular rumor about a dog's saliva being cleaner than a human's mouth? Did you know that's a flat out lie? No basis in reality whatsoever, not one shred of evidence. This myth is spread by delusional folks who enjoy a good lick from their dog.

Do you know what else dog's do with their mouth? They spread disease, fleas, ticks, and bad bacteria. Dogs prefer a bloody, raw, carnivorous diet. They don't shy away from rotten road kill either. You don't have to be animal behavior specialist to know that dogs eat feces and vomit.

They also expel feces, urine, and vomit without warning. They love to chew on furniture, books and my favorite shoes.

Most animals aren't shy about marking their territory either, but God's house isn't their territory. We worship a God who previously mandated animal sacrifices for the remission of sins. With that in mind, we should think twice before we project our personal preferences onto His house of prayer. Some say the solution can be found if we put it up to a vote, but a tyranny of the majority can be just as bad as a tyranny of the minority. Thankfully, God isn't running a democracy. His Kingdom is ruled with love and orderly worship, but the fear of the Lord is in short supply these days.

"Her priests have done violence to My law and have profaned My holy things; they have made no distinction between the holy and the profane, and they have not taught the difference between the unclean and the clean" (Ezekiel 22:26, Leviticus 10:10, Ezekiel 44:23, Zephaniah 3:4)

The Protestant Reformers boldly declared:

Soli Deo gloria - glory to God alone
Solus Christus - through Christ alone
Sola scriptura - by scripture alone
Sola gratia - by grace alone
Sola fide - by faith alone

We reject all of this when we bring our baggage, not to lay at His feet, but as a willful burden that only hinders. We can decide to honor God at church by faith, through Christ alone, carrying only a Bible. This small act of worship only lasts a few hours, (or less) how hard can it be?

What's our alternative choice? If allowed, animals will repeatedly defecate and vomit inside your sanctuary. It's not a matter of if, but when. All theology aside, this is common sense. Even the best dog cannot hold its bladder perfectly, 100% of the time. Every church building rests on holy ground, and every church leader should raise up a high standard.

Consider the following scenario; Your favorite pastor preaches a powerful sermon that moves the congregation to tears. Revival breaks out and you find yourself face down in the carpet, weeping and soaking in sweet presence of the Lord. Christians all over the world will respond at times by prostrating themselves before the Lord. That's normal Christianity. Now I'm supposed to kneel down in the place where your dog drags his anus across the rug? No thanks. Before we move on it's important to ask, how many people in your church are allergic to pet dander?

I just read about a well known church that hosts an annual *Blessings of the Animals* service. Ironically, most of the people who partake in this farce are unaware of it's pagan origins. To offer some perspective, it's typically done before an animal slaughter. Congregants are invited to bring their pets into church so the clergy can pray over them and offer a blessing. Good luck finding that in the Bible. Most Christians have become indistinguishable from the rest of the world.

Please take your doggy devotional service somewhere else. Every church building is the result of hard working, selfless servants who sacrificed a great deal to build and maintain God's house. The founders of your church loved the Lord so much that they worked against incredible odds, and poured themselves out like a drink offering. The only way to honor their efforts is by keeping the church Holy and set apart for ministry.

It's fine to pray for the safety and health of your animals, but conducting a church service that exalts animals is blatantly sacrilegious. How far will this defilement go before the Lord returns? I believe a day is coming when wolves in sheep's clothing will fight for their right to commit bestiality and legally marry themselves to animals inside the church. If permitted, that will be an abomination of desolation. Don't give to dogs what is sacred, don't cast your pearls before swine, and don't fall for the clear and present trend towards licentiousness.

"In 167 B.C. a Greek ruler by the name of Antiochus Epiphanies set up an altar to Zeus over the altar of burnt offerings in the Jewish temple in Jerusalem. He also sacrificed a pig on the altar in the Temple in Jerusalem. This event is known as the abomination of desolation." - GotQuestions.org

Do you love your dogs more than Jesus? Do you love your neighbor? All of eternity hinges on your final answer. Jesus said; "Anyone who loves their father or mother more than me is not worthy of me; anyone who loves their son or daughter more than me is not worthy of me." -Matthew 10:37 NIV

Chapter 8

Who rescued who?

"Greater love hath no man than this, that a man lay down his life for his friends." -John 15:13 KJV

"Every time you humanize your dog and expect him to fulfill the position of an absent child, lover, friend, or parent in your life, you are putting unrealistic expectations on him... you are projecting on him all the emotions, affection, and intimacy

that you lack with the humans in your life."
-Cesar Millan

     Let's peel back another layer from this crazy onion
and dig a little deeper. What if you had to choose between
the life of a dog or a human? It's hard to believe, but a recent
study asked participants to consider the following scenario;
Imagine you discover a house on fire, and you're the first
person on the scene. As you open the door, you hear the
sounds of a child crying and a dog barking in opposite
directions. You're forced to choose between one or the other,
a human or a dog. Who would you save?
     According to an article in *Psychology Today*, "40% of
the subjects said that, under some circumstances... they
would save the animal." I felt sick to my stomach after
reading the results of this research. The further I travel down
this rabbit hole, the crazier it becomes. Under the Old
Covenant, animals were sacrificed for our sins. Today,
people are willing to sacrifice humans for animals. I'm
having a hard time finding rock bottom with idolatry. Here
we find the deepest depths of depravity.
     A few weeks after reading that article in *Psychology
Today* I sat down with a missionary friend who travels to
remote places in Africa to preach in churches and assist with
hands-on volunteer work. He told me a story about a recent
stop at an African airport. While he was waiting for a flight
he had an interesting conversation with a wealthy African
woman who asked about his missionary adventures.
     He shared a few stories about the persecution and
murder of nonviolent Christians, and his efforts to help the
families of innocent martyrs. After a while the wealthy
woman asked my friend how he raised support to pay for his
travel. His said he received part of his funding from churches
in the United States but he mostly relied on odd jobs and day
labor to stay afloat. When she asked about his labors, he told

her about a recent job that involved neutering flocks and herds of livestock for ranchers.

He explained how it was done, with non-surgical, industrial strength castrating bands. At this point the woman became visibly upset. She began chastising and lecturing the young pastor about animal cruelty. How dare he do such a terrible thing to such gentle, unassuming animals? After a few minutes she settled down a bit. My friend asked her; You were upset over goats, but why did you said nothing about the people who are murdered, raped and tortured for their faith?

To her credit, the wealthy woman in the airport realized he was right. She apologized and they parted ways amicably. Most of us would stop what we're doing to help a lost puppy on the side of the road, but how many of us ignore homeless humans on a hot summer day? When we idolize animals (or anything) it's usually in direct proportion to our mistrust of humans. The woman at the airport was somewhat indifferent to human suffering and to be honest, I've done the same at times.

"What good is it, my brothers, if someone says he has faith but does not have works? Can that faith save him? If a brother or sister is poorly clothed and lacking in daily food, and one of you says to them, "Go in peace, be warmed and filled," without giving them the things needed for the body, what good is that? So also faith by itself, if it does not have works, is dead." -James 2:14-17 ESV

I think part of guarding your heart is an intentional effort to resist the urge to become calloused. Can you think of a few practical ways to maintain a tender heart without developing thin skin? This is about operating in the opposite spirit (from what you're feeling), until your feelings catch up with the fact that you have authority in Christ? Some call this faking it until you make it, but that's not what I'm suggesting.

Mind over matter is more accurate. Christians love to talk about moving from head knowledge to heart knowledge, but I'd like to see us take dominion over our tongues. The Apostle Paul said I should beat my body and make it my slave. Other translations put it this way; "I discipline my body and make it my slave, so that, after I have preached to others, I myself will not be disqualified." -1 Corinthians 9:27 NASB However, the Greek word is "hupópiazó: (Strong's 5299) which means to strike under the eye. No pain, no gain indeed.

Much of the Bible flies in the face of secular self help. I've met plenty of people who tried self help for years without a significant breakthrough. They'll try anything except the hardest things like extended times of fasting and prayer. Discipline is good because it liberates you from being a slave to your precious little moods and feelings. If you feel sad, maybe you need rest, but once you're caught up on sleep, try changing your habits to include reading your Bible more often and devoting hours each day to focused worship and praise. "In Your presence is fullness of joy; In Your right hand there are pleasures forever. -Psalm 16:11 NASB

Based on everything I've learned in life, you can't be close to God and remain miserable. You can struggle, suffer, fall down and make mistakes, but if you generally lack joy, then I'd be willing to bet you've drifted away from the Lord. We're always as close to the Lord as we want to be and that's a hard pill to swallow in a world that teaches us to blame everyone except ourselves.

If you feel lonely, call someone and invite them out for a cup of coffee or a game of billiards. Be the change that you want to see in the world, one step at a time. If you know you're coveting hard, do something charitable that costs you money. We drive past the same group of homeless people on our way to work, or a poor family in a trailer park. We walk by certain places hundreds of times without brining an extra bottle of water or a warm blanket.

That's selfish, but before we move on, I'm still trying to wrap my head around the original question at the beginning of this chapter. How far must someone fall before they would save an animal and let a human burn? You aren't likely to walk by a house on fire anytime soon, but every human heart is headed towards a very real, eternal fire apart from the grace of Jesus. (Matthew 10:28) So turn off the TV and set fire to all your "household idols." Turn away from sin and become a laborer in the harvest. If you don't feel a sense of urgency right now, I urge you to take a little extra time to pray today and reconsider your priorities.

Perhaps you've see those black, bone-shaped bumper stickers that ask "who rescued who?" Animals are wonderful but they can't save anyone and you are not their savior. Idolatry happens when we attribute God-like qualities to something or someone other than God. Please take your animals off the pedestal and remember this; 'rescued' is a synonym for saved. Salvation comes through Christ alone. It's heresy to equate dog adoption with anything remotely close to salvation.

Lassie might rescue Timmy from a well, but that's as close as Lassie will come to being his savior. Incidentally, the Bible says animals understand this better than humans. "The ox knows its owner, and the donkey its master's crib, but Israel does not know, my people do not understand." - Isaiah 1:3 ESV

There are plenty of animal lovers who talk about their pets in an almost reverent and mystical manor, and for them it's an idol. The same is true for anyone whose obsessed with a child, lover, or spouse. It doesn't matter if those statements are meant to be figurative or poetic, it's blasphemy. Some will accuse me of going too far, but it's a line that cannot be crossed even with humor, and God knows how much I love a good joke.

Idols cannot save you, but they can destroy you. (Isaiah 45:20 Isaiah 57:13) More importantly, God will not share you with another lover. The Lord isn't trying to be a buzzkill or crash the party, His love will lead you to joy and peace far beyond anything on Earth. Yes, it's an all or nothing proposition from the King of all kings and Lord of lords. Submit to His perfect will and He will pour out blessings beyond measure.

Chapter 9

Worship the Sun or the Son?

"For where your treasure is, there your heart will be also." - Matthew 6:21 NIV

"If the Victorians needed the reminder that natural love is not enough, the old theologians were always saying, very loudly and sternly, that natural love is likely to be a great deal too much. The danger of loving our fellow creatures too little was less present to their minds than that of loving them idolatrously. In every wife, mother, child, and friend, they saw a possible rival to God, and so of coarse does our Lord. " -C.S. Lewis

A few months ago I was out running errands when a full-grown Blue Heeler tried to attack my three-year-old daughter. We were walking into a large retail store in a wealthy neighborhood. The dog's owner was barely able to hold her leash when that big dog started barking wildly and lunging at my toddler. It was exhibiting redline rage and could have seriously injured or killed my thirty-pound daughter within seconds.

I've seen dogs fight and nip at each other in public but there's no excuse for any amount of threatening behavior towards humans, especially children. Be on your guard beloved, the days are growing darker. It's safe to assume that this dog owner knew her Heeler was unpredictable and dangerous. Things like this rarely happen without prior warning signs. I suspect this was not the first outburst of rage from her precious fur baby. She was visibly embarrassment, but didn't seem to be surprised.

We were not walking towards the dog, and gave it plenty of space, but that shouldn't matter. Even if a kid walks straight up to a dog and enthusiastically greets it without permission, the dog owner is 100% liable for whatever happens. Common sense says keep your dog at home if there's any doubt. If your animal hurts a human, you're looking at possible jail time and a costly lawsuit. A legal battle could ruin your finances, and it's more common than you might think. We will cover that more in chapter 9.

Saying sorry in a situation like this is disingenuous at best because that dog owner should have known better. It's similar to the mindset of a big guy who mumbles an apology while he rudely shoves past you in a crowded space. Any sane person would doubt the sincerity of such apologies, if anything, the offender regrets being embarrassed.

Right and wrong are as plain as day if you're walking with the Lord, as Children of the light. So let's set the record straight once and for all. Your dog is not a person, pets are not people. The mainstream media has surrounded us with an endless barrage of loud lies, and keeping yourself free from deception requires determination.

Human life is precious and fragile, it must be guarded fiercely. It seems ironic to me, but I know anti-gun people who buy large, powerful, and unruly guard dogs. Many dog owners lack the physical strength that's required to keep their powerful dogs under control.

"Therefore, holy brothers and sisters, who share in the heavenly calling, fix your thoughts on Jesus... Jesus has been found worthy of greater honor than Moses, just as the builder of a house has greater honor than the house itself. For every house is built by someone, but God is the builder of everything." -Hebrews 3:1-4 NIV

"81% of those surveyed consider their dogs to be true family members, equal in status to children." -Psychology Today

I moved to Southern California a few years after dropping out of college. After watching so many movies that idolized Hollywood, I was eager to experience warmer weather and better career opportunities. Finding work was easy and I had a great time overall. During that time I had the privilege of befriending and working with many brilliant individuals from around the world. Los Angeles is an incredibly diverse melting pot and I would probably still there if the state and local laws weren't so crazy.

I love reading even more than writing. As such, I've always loved libraries and local book stores. One day, when I was working in Santa Monica, I wandered into a dusty old book shop and started flipping through vintage magazines. I specifically remember reading about the ancient practice of sun worship in Egypt. It's funny because later that day I went on a walk with a friend along the boardwalk and most of the beach-goers were essentially worshipping the sun.

In the sunshine state, locals and tourists alike would flock to the beach whenever the weather permitted. By Kansas standards, it's pretty much always nice there, so I made the most out of it and took daily walks along the beach after work, or on my lunch break. Each day I passed the same groups of camera-toting tourists and leather-skinned locals, diligently soaking up the sun while playing sand volleyball or laying on the sand.

Tourists from around the world joyfully frolicked in the water, even when the locals wore winter coats and complained about temperatures below 60 degrees. I love going to the beach with friends or by myself to pray. There's nothing wrong with a day at the beach but people tend to worship creation itself, instead of the creator. Humans prefer to worship what we can touch and see, but we don't call it worship. We call it something else, anything else, preferring to see ourselves as connoisseurs or aficionados, anything other than idolaters.

The Egyptians had plenty of other gods besides the sun itself. In ancient Egypt, cats were worshiped as divine creatures and today they are worshipped nearly everywhere I travel. So many of us pray for prosperity, but hoarding great wealth has caused more harm than good to individuals with even the best intentions.

Only a few hundred years ago it was illegal to own certain breeds of dogs or cats that were favored by royalty. I've heard about kings and queens who were murderously obsessive about their favorite animals. Back then you could be executed or thrown in prison for daring to break the royal doggy decrees.

I guess there's nothing new under the sun because I've seen pet owners practically come to blows while defending their dog in public. In the modern era, our affluence has led to a glut of wealthy pseudo-princes and princesses who prefer to view themselves as average middle-class folks. We pretend as if we are not rich, and in many cases, all the evidence in the world can't change a rebellious heart.

If you've never read the book *Rich Christians in an Age of Hunger*, by Ronald J. Sider, please check it out. I wish everyone would invest a few hours into this eye-opening modern classic. Spoiler alert; Most of us are rich by any meaningful standard, but we deny it because that would make us liable for every Biblical warning, woe and rebuke that's directed at the rich. For example; "woe to you who are rich, for you have already received your comfort." -Luke 6:24 NIV

Christians must uphold a higher standard and resist the deceitfulness of wealth. We can't bow down to anyone but God. Deep down inside everyone knows it's wrong to kill a baby, and if you stop to think about what the Lord has done in your life, you won't downplay the favor, advantages and abundant blessings in your life. We cannot redefine words to suit our moods. Instead, let's have the courage to face reality and stand for the truth, even when it hurts.

"the cares of the world and the deceitfulness of riches and the desires for other things enter in and choke the word, and it proves unfruitful." -Mark 4:19 ESV

"Adopting a pet from an animal shelter costs $50 to $100, and that's just the start. Between food and veterinarian care, you're looking at $500 a year. And that's if you treat Fido like a mutt. If you want to treat your dog or cat like you'd want to be treated, you'll need to throw in toys, flea-and-tick treatments, grooming, and a nice bed. That can add up to $1,500 to $2,000 a year. If you want to treat your pet like royalty, you'll shovel money for stuff like teeth cleanings, professional training, boarding and even $2,000 cataract surgery when they get old. All told, the annual cost could be $10,350, according to Petfinder.com. You can spend 1/10th of that and Fido will still love you. -Debt.org

How much would you pay to acquire your favorite animal? The total cost of ownership stretches far beyond the price tag for any specific breed. In fact, it can be a bit like owning a race car where the total cost over time is far greater than the purchase price. You might be able to buy a race car, but that doesn't mean you can afford to keep it up and running. It's also fair to point out the fact that most vehicles, yes even sports cars, are bought with borrowed money.

A friend of mine is a mechanic at a large Mercedes Benz dealership in California. According to his experience, when someone pulls up to his shop with an entry-level, C-Class Mercedes, his team will instinctively brace themselves for the possibility of a conflict. Why? They know the owner is likely to complain and argue about the cost of parts and maintenance.

On the other hand, when a customer pulls up in a top of the line S-Class, everyone smiles and breathes a sigh of relief. With few exceptions, the truly wealthy clients aren't overly concerned about the time or money that's required to upkeep their cars because they are living within their means. This isn't an endorsement or condemnation of German luxury cars, it's simply an observation. Fast cars are fun and exciting, but if you feel like you need to buy expensive stuff to impress your friends or improve your social status, then you don't understand your identity in Christ, the dangers of covetousness, or the importance of the ministry.

When I was little, a pedigree Labrador Retriever with good papers cost around three hundred dollars. It was a bit pricey, but not unreasonable. Today, inflation has taken its toll and consumer demand is high. The most popular breeds start around two thousand dollars, but it's not unheard of to pay ten thousand dollars for a puppy.

That's a staggering amount of money, but even the most expensive dog cannot compare to the price of a prized pony. Pure breed puppies are notorious for health issues due to the disgusting practice of inbreeding. I'm not a fan of puppy mills, but even if you adopt from a shelter, the cost of veterinarian care can quickly drain the average person's bank account.

If you can't afford a dream dog, there are plenty of shops that will finance the purchase of your favorite K9 status symbol. Most veterinarian clinics offer a third party line of credit if you're able to qualify. When the Vet offers financing, it puts pressure on the customers. It's hard to say no when the financing company indirectly implies that you're a heartless monster if you refuse their services.

The interest rates can be excessive if you don't pay off your loan quickly. Does any of this seem unreasonable? The true cost of ownership forces thousands of animal lovers to surrender or abandon their pets every year.

Meanwhile, big-box pet stores are strategically designed to tempt you with a wide variety of impulse purchases. That's why you have to walk so far to find dog food and kitty litter. Department stores sell expensive doggy purses and strollers that will set you back a few hundred dollars, but the most exclusive designers offer bespoke doggy handbags for ten thousand dollars or more.

Have you ever been to the Kentucky Derby? How about a Greyhound racing track? The amount of money that's squandered at race tracks is staggering, and I'm not talking about fancy hats or mint juleps. Hundreds of billions of dollars are wagered by gamblers every year, but the house always wins in the end. Gambling addicts call their addiction gaming, as if they were enjoying a friendly game of checkers or chess. They're like delusional abortion advocates who prefer to use the word fetus while discussing a pre-born baby.

Fetus is Latin for baby, but hardly anyone understands Latin. In reality, they're using puffed-up terminology to distance themselves from the ugly truth. It's an intentionally deceptive marketing strategy. Abortionists say fetus in an attempt to control the discussion by re-defining the terms. It's easier to shirk responsibility when you make up your own rules or change the rules to suit your argument. Alcohol and tobacco manufactures do the same with fancy, ornate packaging.

Overall, wealthy Equestrians take the cake when it comes to frivolous spending. Elite breeders use custom outfitted, 'equine equipped' private jets to transport their best horses. Chartering one will set you back thousands of dollars per hour depending on the size and capabilities of the jet. Most of us can't afford first-class plane tickets, let alone a fully staffed, multi-million dollar Gulfstream. We all seek comfort in one way or another. Some of us love the roar of the crowd, others prefer a cozy loveseat. As a frequent traveler, I've spent a lot of time in airport terminals but I've never flown on a private jet or paid to sit in first class.

From a business perspective, it makes sense considering the astronomical figures associated with elite horse racing and breeding. A champion stallion can earn $150,000 or more for sewing his seed. The most in-demand stud earned thirty-five million dollars in 2017. Where does all this money come from? Some of it can be attributed to wasteful millionaires who flaunt their fortunes, but the bulk comes from middle-class spectators and gamblers.

That's also true with leagues like the NBA or NFL. Most professional sports organizations have millions of fans lined up to pay $100 for tickets and $40 for an officially licensed t-shirt. We don't pay to watch gladiators die in the ring anymore, but countless lives have been destroyed on the altar of sports idolatry. I love a good game as much as the next guy, and it's possible for you to enjoy a football season without worshipping athletes or their accomplishments.

Dog references in the Bible

How often are dogs mentioned in the Bible and what's the context? Before we move on, let's look at what the Bible says about dogs. Please take a moment to read through a few of these examples, please read the whole chapter and/or story for context.

Dogs » Described as » Carnivorous » 1 Kings 14:11, 2 Kings 9:36

Dogs » Illustrative » Of **obstinate sinners** » Matthew 7:6, Revelation 22:15

Dogs » Illustrative » Of dead » 1 Samuel 24:14, 2 Samuel 9:8

Dogs » Illustrative » Of gentiles » Matthew 15:22,26

Dogs » Described as » **Fond of blood** » 1 Kings 22:38, 1 Kings 21:19

Dogs » Nothing holy to be given to » Matthew 7:6, and 15:26

Dogs » Illustrative » Of **persecutors** » Psalms 22:16,20

Dogs » Described as » **Unclean** » Luke 16:21, 2 Peter 2:22

Dogs » Price of, not to be consecrated » Deuteronomy 23:18

Dogs » Illustrative » Of **false teachers** » Philippians 3:2

Dogs » Illustrative » Of **fools** » Proverbs 26:11

Dogs » Described as » Impatient of injury » Proverbs 26:17

Dogs » Infested cities by night » Psalm 59:14-15

Dogs » Illustrative » of **unfaithful ministers** » Isaiah 56:10

Dogs » Illustrative » Of **covetous ministers** » Isaiah 56:11

Dogs » Illustrative » Of **apostates** » 2 Peter 2:22

Dogs » Things torn by beasts given to » Exodus 22:31

Dogs » Despised by the jews » 2 Samuel 3:8

Dogs » Described as » **Dangerous and destructive** » Psalm 22:16

Dogs » Sacrificing of, **an abomination** » Isaiah 66:3

Dogs » Manner of, in drinking, alluded to » Judges 7:5

Dogs » **A term of reproach** » Philippians 3:2, Matthew 7:6, Matthew 15:26, Revelation 22:15

Dogs » Names » **Of the wicked** » Revelation 22:15

Dogs » **Wicked people** » Compared with » Matthew 7:6, 2 Peter 2:22, Proverbs 26:11

(Source; Thematic Bible https://bible.knowing-jesus.com/topics/Dogs)

Chapter 7

Dogs and crumbs

"He answered, "I was sent only to the lost sheep of the house
of Israel." But she came and knelt before him, saying, "Lord,
help me." And he answered, "It is not right to take the
children's bread and throw it to the dogs." She said, "Yes,
Lord, yet even the dogs eat the crumbs that fall from their
masters' table." Then Jesus answered her, "O woman, great is
your faith! Be it done for you as you desire." And her
daughter was healed instantly." -Matthew 15:21-28 ESV

""Dogs," as referred to in this text, were a metaphor in the
first century for those who repented and embraced the cross,
and then returned to their sinful lives just as dogs return to
their vomit. Such are assigned their lot with the evil ones." -
Rick Joyner

    If you're worried about the eternal fate of your pets,
you will be relieved to know that Walt Disney settled the
matter years ago with the hit movie *All Dogs Go to Heaven*.
Earth is only a shadow of Heaven, and I believe that
wholeheartedly. You can rest easy knowing that Fido will
join you in Heaven, but the fate of your human neighbors is
far less certain. In our Father's house, there will be no pain,
thieves or death. Jesus will wipe away every tear from your
eyes and we will no longer recall the former things. (Isaiah
65:17)

    How do you think God feels about dogs after reading

those verses? The only choice now is to decide if you believe what's written. The way you live your life is your answer. If you aren't sure how dogs fit into the language of the Holy Bible, just read it, don't take my word. God loves all of creation, but it's His will that we keep everything within a proper perspective. Orderliness does not diminish love at all, it honors God. Dogs are a gift from God, but He alone is worthy of our praise.

Whenever someone is compared to a dog in the Bible, it's a stern rebuke or a final judgment. In the Bible, false teachers are compared to dogs, and that's intended to be an insult. Overall, when a dog is mentioned in the Bible, it's always an extremely unflattering context. That's true for both the Old and New Testament. Contrary to what some say, God does use harsh language at times, and since He is God, all of His judgments are perfect. (Revelation 16:7 Psalm 119:160)

Whether we're talking about Jezebel, or Jesus and the Canaanite woman, it's hard to miss the punchline when dogs are the butt of the joke. No disrespect intended, so don't shoot the messenger when I say God has been greatly disrespected by our irreverence and overall lack of dignity and honor. We don't have a problem with calling God our Father or a friend, but we struggle mightily with His Lordship. He's the boss, and that's great news.

Before moving on, let's take a moment to consider the story of the faithful mother from Mark 7 and Matthew 15. She could have decided to take offense at the "dogs and crumbs" comment from Jesus and walked away with nothing. Thank God, that's not how her story ended, and I'm happy to say your story isn't over yet either.

What can we learn from this seemingly harsh parable? First, let's state the obvious; this was a real tough test for a desperate mother, and she showed great humility. We don't know what tone of voice Jesus used, but it was loving. Remember, true love doesn't always look or sound like Hollywood romance movies. I know I would have a hard time with that little jab about "feeding the dogs". However, this long-suffering mother received instant deliverance for her "cruelly demon-possessed" daughter as a direct result of her response.

Have you ever wondered what would've happened if she had reacted with anger or so-called righteous indignation? Would her daughter have been set free from the torment that afflicted her entire community? It's doubtful, especially when considering what happened when the Son of Man visited His hometown of Nazareth (Matthew 13:57). The Jews He grew up with "esteemed Him lightly" (1 Samuel 2:30).

Those who thought they knew Him rejected their one true Messiah due to an overly-assumptive familiarity. In short, they failed the attitude test while the Canaanite woman handled it magnificently. The same is true for those who walked away when Jesus started talking about eating His flesh and drinking His blood. (John 6:61-6:67) Does this offend you? Your response to adversity reveals the condition of your heart, "blessed is the one who is not offended by me." -Matthew 11:6 ESV

You might go to church and know all about God, maybe you've read hundreds of theology books while attending the best schools. Then again, it's possible to do all that and more without ever truly following Christ. Real love is the only meaningful hallmark. Do you love your neighbor? You never know who God might use to deliver an important message, but that's OK if you learn to recognize His voice. If you become overly familiar, like the townsfolk of Nazareth, then you might miss Him altogether. "Therefore let him who thinks he stands take heed that he does not fall." -1 Corinthians 10:12 NASB

God gave dominion over every creature on Earth to mankind (Genesis 1:26-28) and we are still responsible as stewards over creation today. In light of the glorious gift of eternal salvation, the only appropriate response is plundering hell to populate heaven. The wedding feast that Jesus spoke about often is rapidly approaching, wouldn't you like to see more people saved as a direct result of your relationships?

Life is full of many little tests and a few big ones. In each experience, God is the constant, and we are the variable. We fall short, but God never fails, He is always faithful. The way we respond to "trials of many kinds" (James 1:2-4) reveals the substance of our faith. The Ark of salvation is a gift for all who believe. Do you care enough to help your neighbors onto the Ark? Many of our neighbors are drowning in sin and sorrow, they need your help. The Great Commission was given for everyone who joins in this labor, as fishers of men. It all points back to love so lets "Love thy neighbor" (not thy dog) "as thyself". (Mark 12:31)

Chapter 8

How much is too much?

Headlines:

"The Insane Battle Over Sam Simon's Will - Should the 'Simpsons' Co-Creator's Trust Pay $140,000 Per Year for One Dog's Care?' -The Hollywood Reporter

"Simon was spending about $140,000 annually on the troubled but clearly well-loved animal, including $7,500 a month on almost daily training and more than $3,500 (also a month!) on twice-weekly acupuncture sessions... he would need between $1 million and $2 million to care for the dog over time." -Slate

"So if you have not been trustworthy in handling worldly wealth, who will trust you with true riches?" -Luke 16:11 NIV

Whenever I have discussions about idolatry the conversation eventually turns to the question of how much is too much? An old pastor once told me that it's foolish to see how close you can get to sin without actually sinning. I think that's a great way to explain the seemingly abstract issue of liberty. I want to do something, but is it beneficial? That's a far better question than simply asking if something is permissible. (1 Corinthians 6:12, 10:23)

When believers mature beyond the starting point of spiritual infancy, we begin to ask what's best instead of trying to justify whatever it is we prefer to do. The next question is how should you define moderation? Western Christians aren't always taught moderation, at least, not from what I've seen. We are given a long list of rules (based on our denomination, regional differences and ethnic groups).

At the top of this chapter are two headlines that caught my attention shortly after the death of *The Simpsons* co-creator, Sam Simon. To be fair, (and life is not fair) Simon's net worth was around one hundred million dollars at the time of his death. Do you think it's God's will for you or anyone to waste millions on one dog? I'm starting with an extreme example, but we have to start somewhere in the oft-neglected conversation of moderation.

OK, how about this; would you justify some kind of 'Mary of Bethany' alabaster jar moment for a terminal old dog? Is it OK to pour out a year's salary on the paws of your beloved golden retriever before they are euthanized at the vet? How much is too much? When I asked a group of friends about Sam Simon's dog, their opinions varied drastically. I was in the process of writing this book when it happened, so I asked about this situation specifically, for a little anecdotal research.

Most of the feedback was predictable, they viewed such lavish spending as excessive and unreasonable. Others saw it as no big deal, let the guy do what he wants with his vast wealth and let poor people be damned. How does God feel about this situation? The Bible has plenty to say about money, and it's easy to understand.

Yikes, I don't want God to say that to me on judgment day, how about you? It's also true that Jesus mentions money over a dozen times. His parables reveal the motives of our hearts. The decisions we make with money reveals our hearts. What else did Jesus say about money? If you aren't sure, start with these passages; (Mark 10:17-27, Mark 4:19, Luke 16:14-15).

Two thousand years ago, if you wanted to follow Christ during His brief ministry on Earth, you would have had to physically follow Him in person. You couldn't just click here to subscribe or watch His new video series online. His disciples often slept on the ground in the winter. They dropped everything to travel for years without giving notice.

The fickle masses would line up to watch Him preach, but there were a faithful few who never left His side. In three years they walked hundreds of miles in sandals through rainstorms, scorching hot wastelands, and busy city streets. Back then you couldn't just drive to your favorite church in a safe, climate-controlled building. True devotion to His Kingdom will always be risky and costly.

The book of James warns against living in luxury, (ch 5) but how do you define luxury? That's a tough question but it's one that must be answered. It's better to judge yourself now, I don't want to be surprised when God judges me according to my faith and His word. We know it's wrong to store up treasure on earth, (Matthew 6:19-21) but I've seen so many Christians engaging in conspicuous consumption.

"In 2010 Americans spent over 47 Billion dollars on their pets, this amount has more than doubled since the 1998 expense of 23 Billion... The American Pet Products Association estimates $60.59 billion will be spent on pets in 2015" -APPA

At work, it feels like I'm surrounded by talented, well-educated Christians who chase money nonstop. In other places, I see talented, well-educated Christians who refuse to work a full-time job, as if that would crush their soul. Both groups should know better, and both can talk a good game when it comes to spirituality. Guys, can we talk about moderation for goodness sake? God isn't a relativist and His ways are higher than our ways.

Everyone will be judged by a fair and impartial standard. Even if you're a brain-dead dummy, that's OK, God uses a sliding scale. What you have in terms of talents, is more than enough to run your race in such a way as to win the prize. You don't need piles of money to be a blessing, (or to please God) that's a lie. God gives seed to the sower and if the seed doesn't seem to be forthcoming, it's time to look at what you're doing with what you've been given. You don't need a dream job to fulfill your highest purpose and calling, so start small and resist the urge to despise your humble beginnings.

Throughout much of human history, any saint who spoke up for Christ was likely to be imprisoned, tortured and then murdered. Christianity wasn't a social status booster like it is in some places today. Book stores are overflowing with bestsellers from big-name pastors who constantly rehash the same handful of self-serving themes of health, wealth, greasy grace, and financial prosperity "above all things". It's very popular but that doesn't make it right.

Beloved, these played-out themes have been rehashed

so many times because they're cash cows. Don't fall for it anymore, you are smart enough to know better. They begin with partial truths, but their sketchy foundations represent (at best) one percent of the entire Bible. It's always the same handful of cherry-picked scriptures and they intentionally neglect anything else from the Bible that might offer balance or clarity. "Fools base their thoughts on foolish assumptions, so their conclusions will be wicked madness;" -Ecclesiastes 10:13 NLT

Wolves in sheep's clothing are those who extract a Bible verse in the same way high fructose corn syrup is derived from the syrup of a corn plant. It's the sweetest possible extract, a fragment of a fragment, and it's a carefully crafted, nefarious strategy to supplant a healthy, well-balanced meal. Most pastors are humble, modest and selfless, but life is fragile, it doesn't take much effort to poison a well. "one sinner destroys much good." -Ecclesiastes 9:18

When an overly ambitious preacher starts with the goal of getting rich off the Gospel, you can be sure it will end badly for everyone involved. The wrong path never becomes the right path, no matter how long you stay on that road. Unless that fool changes his course, it will only lead to wicked madness.

There must be a million self-centered, self-help books in the Christian genre, but you won't find any of that garbage inside a classic, antique Christian book. The past generations were far from perfect, but from what I've read, they put us to shame with their discipline, work ethic, integrity, and community. Don't take my word for it, be like the noble Bereans who weren't afraid of a little research. (Acts 17:11)

You could search through an entire library of dusty, old, out of print Christian books and struggle to find one page of the superficial, cotton candy that's popular today. When did mainstream publishers fall off the wagon? In America, a major shift in theology began in the nineteen sixties. Ivy Universities and small-town community colleges were slowly, methodically infiltrated by god-hating teachers and students who pursued advanced degrees in theology for all the wrong reasons.

'Know thy enemy' was their motto. By the nineteen-eighties, the inmates were running the madhouse, aka, major media and publishing companies. Since then it's more common to find spiritual milk and shallow Christian truths mixed with new-age nonsense. There are plenty of excellent books in circulation right now, but the bulk of the profits are gobbled up by books that sprinkle in a few Bible verses in the same way an online marketer carefully embeds trendy keywords into a website.

Each chapter is lightly seasoned with Christian lingo for good effect and everyone at church will call you a troublemaker (behind your back) if you dare to question the new normal. I've read books that claimed to be about the Bible but they didn't contain a single quote from the Bible. What would the Apostle Paul say about our bizarre situation? "for I did not shrink from declaring to you the whole counsel of God." -Acts 20:27 ESV

What is the whole council, or, as some translations say, the whole purpose of God? That's the big picture and the small details. It's the full Gospel, not just your favorite parts. It's good news and a bunch of sobering warnings. So embrace the challenging and difficult parts of the Bible, not just the touchy-feely stuff that fits nicely in holiday greeting cards. How much is too much? We will explore this more in the second half of this book. "Examine yourselves, to see whether you are in the faith. Test yourselves. Or do you not realize this about yourselves, that Jesus Christ is in you?— unless indeed you fail to meet the test!" -2 Corinthians 13:5 ESV

Chapter 9

How much is too little?

"Pure and undefiled religion in the sight of our God and Father is this: to visit orphans and widows in their distress, and to keep oneself unstained by the world." -James 1:27 NASB

"Do you know there are people out there who have ministries to animals because they can't deal with people? I would tell you, that's not very good. Animals can't talk back, that's why people love animals so much because there are no issues. But you are here because you are somebody's solution."
-Todd White

How much is too little when it comes to your kids or animals? In the strictest sense, I've rarely witnessed neglect first hand. It seemed rare because it was well hidden. Explosive verbal abuse was far more common. The world teaches us to use positive reinforcement and nothing else, but if you offend the "thought police" of political correctness, they will metaphorically go for your throat like a rabid Rottweiler. How's that for positive reinforcement?

There are many ways the enemy can destroy the defenseless without using physical force. How much is too much? Abuse is always too much. How much is too little? Negligence, passivity, and cowardice are not enough for real Christians. We all make mistakes, but there's a big gap between a dictatorship and total anarchy. A lack of discipline leads to the necessity of punishment, and you don't have to be super-spiritual to understand natural consequences. If you play with hell's fire long enough, you will burn.

The wisdom of Christ was given to avoid unnecessary troubles and heartaches. Only God can see the end from the beginning. The Lord isn't legalistic, He isn't waiting around for you to slip up just so He can punish you. Grace is the only reason I'm still alive. The Lord sanctifies His Children despite our failures. Why does God seem so strict? Well, there's no positive reinforcement in prison or hell.

God allows difficult circumstances to prepare you for a very long eternity, but He's also willing to prepare you for upcoming challenges this week. When you realize who you are in Heaven, you'll be much more useful here on Earth. We all fail at times, but would you rather fail because you never tried hard enough, or is it better to fail because you occasionally tried too hard? "Do not be excessively wicked and do not be a fool. Why should you die before your time?" -Ecclesiastes 7:17 NASB

Discipline is the path to freedom. Why? Because poorly behaved kids fair much worse in life and unruly pets end up in the hands of animal control officers. Most dog shelters cannot afford the luxury of a no-kill policy and in case you didn't know it, most prisons do a lousy job when it comes to rehabilitation. That may hard to accept, but it's easy to understand. Euthanasia is a real risk for unruly pets, and that's just another reason why tough love does not equal abuse, even if it's unpleasant. Why should you (or your dog) die before your time?

It's helpful and life-giving to judiciously spank a child or swat a dog at times, and yes, the Bible's lessons on corporal punishment are trustworthy. You can sparingly punish a child without reveling in the spirit of anger or inflicting emotional trauma. It's not the solution to every problem, and it only works up to a point. "Let the godly strike me! It will be a kindness! If they correct me, it is soothing medicine. Don't let me refuse it. But I pray constantly against the wicked and their deeds." -Psalm 141:5

NLT

Physical pain is a teacher whether we like it or not. Your commitment to tough love might be exactly what's needed to pull someone away from a path of violence. Some kids become violent as a result of being abused, but it's also likely for neglected children. Both fire and ice can burn the skin, so let's avoid each extreme. In our next chapter, we will discuss what happens when animals are abused and neglected.

You might have bad memories of harsh leaders who abused verses like this; "spare the rod, spoil the child", but their failure does not prove the Bible wrong. The answer to misuse isn't non-use but proper use. The world says people are basically good, but God has assured us that "The heart is deceitful above all things, and desperately sick; who can understand it?" -Jeremiah 17:9 ESV

At times it's helpful to state the obvious. Child abuse and animal cruelty are evil. Coincidentally, both of these evil deeds have been illegal for a long time. Interesting side note; violent criminals aren't concerned about the law, nor do they care when another new law is passed. What did the Bible teach us about relying on the law? Rules and regulations can't change the heart, the Old Covenant proved that once and for all.

The New Covenant is our only hope. So let's warm our hearts by the fire of Christ and embrace His baptism of fire until we glow like beacons of light, shining bright in the darkest night. "Therefore we do not lose heart. Though outwardly we are wasting away, yet inwardly we are being renewed day by day. For our light and momentary troubles are achieving for us an eternal glory that far outweighs them all." -2 Corinthians 4:16,17 NIV

When I was a dog trainer, I ran into the politically correct idol of positive reinforcement. The employees at my pet store treated the subject like a sacred cow and that doctrine became an idol. You were accepted or rejected based on your acceptance of their unquestionable dogma. In our obedience classes, we had a strict rule that prohibited trainers from doing anything that could be interpreted by customers as discipline or correction.

The fear of one extreme (abuse) unintentionally led to the opposite extreme of passivity. Parents often do the same thing with their children. I've met plenty who are overly controlling "helicopter parents" while others lean back and opt for a hands-off approach. Some parents are abusive and overbearing while others refuse to hold their kids accountable for their worst actions.

"It is good to grasp the one and not let go of the other. Whoever fears God will avoid all extremes." -Ecclesiastes 7:18 NIV

"I feel a strong desire to tell you - and I expect you feel a strong desire to tell me - which of these two errors is the worse. That is the devil getting at us. He always sends errors into the world in pairs - pairs of opposites. And he always encourages us to spend a lot of time thinking which is the worse. You see why, of course? He relies on your extra dislike of the one error to draw you gradually into the opposite one. But do not let us be fooled. We have to keep our eyes on the goal and go straight through between both errors. We have no other concern than that with either of them." -C.S. Lewis

The NASB translation phrases it this way: "It is good that you grasp one thing and also not let go of the other; for the one who fears God comes forth with both of them." I like both versions because they both say the same thing in a slightly different way. It's easy to see extremism usually leads to absurdities and insanity. In my pet store we could only use methods with 100% positive reinforcement. If anything in class could be interpreted as negative reinforcement or positive punishment, it was off-limits. Most of the time we worked with gentle, smaller breeds. Basic commands were taught, dog treats were dispensed liberally, and cute puppies were paraded up and down the aisles.

The difficult dogs were ignored if they were little, or banned from class if they were large. A teacup Terrier could run around biting our ankles, but we would never swat a dog with a rolled-up newspaper or squirt them with a water bottle. (my preferred discipline methods) We offered excellent customer service, which humans enjoy, but even five-star service has little effect on difficult dogs. Our class would usually come under control with exercise, but the worst offenders needed more than what we had to offer.

Almost every day we'd have one or two dogs that made everything harder for everyone. They were edgy, overly hyper, and extremely difficult. The pet owners were full of excuses and apologies but also holding on for dear life. We just wanted to help them avoid a one way trip to the animal shelter. Behavioral problems are no laughing matter, thousands of dogs are euthanized every year due to a lack of discipline.

In a perfect world, our students would take their dogs outside, practice what we taught them, and get plenty of exercise. Classes would be fun and everyone would excel. Experienced trainers know that difficult animals come with the territory, it's called work for a reason. Most teaching methods offer a great deal of repetition, but no one enjoys starting from scratch with the same dogs over and over again. None of us were getting rich from selling dog lessons, and that's why even a small victory in obedience was valued more than the money earned from repeat business.

The behavioral problems we encountered revealed the attitudes of our pet owners. There seemed to be a total disconnect between cause and effect. The same is true for human parents. I know who are against spanking, but the run around in circles all day, constantly arguing with tyrannical toddlers and treacherous teenagers. You can't negotiate with terrorists, and little kids are the main reason I embraced the doctrine of total depravity.

What would rather do; have a house full of peace with the occasional, even-tempered swat, or will you endure never-ending debates with a pint-sized four-year-old? You can fight for your new normal if it makes you feel good, but many of our modern problems were virtually unknown in past generations. It's just another sign of the times. If you think I'm exaggerating, perhaps you're life is like the frog in the water that's lulled to sleep as it slowly heats up to a rolling boil.

Whoever heard of an old farmer with an anxious ranch dog? Impossible, but in big cities, cramped living spaces and overly ambitious career paths, it's par for the course. Some environments aren't good for a dog. So don't be afraid to admit when you're in trouble. Just ask for help and correct the situation. My customers were happy to pay for lessons and eager to earn certificates, but I'd guess that maybe half of those pups didn't receive training or discipline at home. Instead, they were left alone throughout the week without much exercise or access to a decent sized yard. The pet owners I met would confess to being overworked and overcommitted. As a result, they kenneled their dogs at home to the point of negligence.

Even so, I have to give credit where it's due. At least these pet owners were making an effort to improve their situation by seeking our help. They paid for lessons and took the time to attend obedience classes, which is a big step in the right direction. As a new trainer, I was full of enthusiasm and high hopes, but after observing a few of the top trainers in my region, I was disappointed, to say the least.

Our regional experts didn't seem to be overly concerned with producing results as much as looking good and sounding smart. They preferred to focus on schmoozing and it worked like a charm. These were the rockstar trainers in our organization who had stellar reputations. After a few weeks, I longed to work at an independent dog training academy. Instead, I was stuck at a big-box store that focused on profit, people-pleasing, and politicking. When it came to actual training, we didn't see great results, it was lukewarm at best.

I can't fault them for doing what they thought was best, but it felt like a high school popularity contest with little substance. The big shots in our training program were all about keeping up appearances. To them, positive emotional takeaways were valued above all else. It's idolatry, but you wouldn't know it unless you take time to study the Bible, or if you're lucky enough to sit under of those rare teaching pastors who is both unafraid and intelligent.

The top trainers in my market understood the game they were playing. They'd go out of their way to fabricate special moments without making it feel fake or corny. Like a skillful actor or a con artist, they sought out opportunities to stroke a customer's ego just enough without being obvious. In my place of business, the feel was always more important than the real.

If I had to put a fine point on it, the greatest skill among our top performers was either flattery or manipulation. Right now you might be wondering if I'm being fair, but consider this; if people-pleasing is our primary focus, then the worst thing anyone can do is offend someone. Christ commands us to speak the truth in love, in all circumstances, even when it's offensive. "For the message of the cross is foolishness to those who are perishing, but to us who are being saved it is the power of God."
- 1 Corinthians 1:18 NIV

That's why it's so important for Christians to focus on pleasing God rather than man. It's a conflict that forces the decision, you can't pick both. Even if you're most diplomatic person on earth, you will offend those who have rejected Christ; "am I now seeking the approval of man, or of God?

Or am I trying to please man? If I were still trying to please man, I would not be a servant of Christ." -Galatians 1:10 ESV

The spirit of political correctness is the counterfeit of true, biblical grace. The Word of God must be your straight edge and measuring tape. As we've discussed in previous chapters, humans naturally drift towards extremes. That includes worshipping our ever-changing moods and feelings. Humility is God's solution to this age-old problem. If we don't think too highly of ourselves then it's impossible to elevate our precious little opinions above God's higher way.

Fear the Lord, and choose the path of a bondservant for Christ. I promise that it's easier than whatever else you're trying. Society has embraced a PC culture that demands obedience in ways that stretch far beyond any reasonable rules of social etiquette or decorum. The enemy craves control because you are easier to defeat when you're worried about following a bunch of man-made rules that came from the devil. "But even if we or an angel from heaven should preach to you a gospel contrary to the one we preached to you, let him be accursed." -Galatians 1:8 ESV

I could write a large book about the insanity of political correctness, but it's sufficient to say that making an idol out of emotions is heresy. What else would you call the rejection of God's sovereignty? Jesus Christ will only ever lead you away from the spirit of control; "It was for freedom that Christ set us free; therefore keep standing firm and do not be subject again to a yoke of slavery." -Galatians 5:1 NASB

You cannot take up your daily cross and live in fear of the world at the same time. If you reckon yourselves to be dead indeed to sin, then you've got nothing to lose and everything to gain. It's also impossible to chase the shifting sands and trends of this world while standing firm on the foundation of Christ Jesus. Everyone struggles with fear, but don't let it control your life.

How much is too much and how much is too little? Seek the Lord while He may be found and let His light guide you. (Isaiah 55:6) There's a balance to strike between being polite and standing for the truth with boldness. It's good to care what others think. That's called being considerate, but don't let the approval of others rule your life.

The Apostle Paul worked hard as he served remote churches in the first century, but he wasn't trying to win a popularity contest. There are times when the most loving choice is a sharp rebuke. (Titus 1:3) Those times are rare, but it should never be off the table entirely. Forget what the world says, discipline is beneficial. God disciplines those He loves, and a well-timed swat from a rolled-up newspaper is not as bad as it sounds. (Proverbs 23:13)

Chapter 10

The dark side of puppy love

The righteous care for the needs of their animals, but the kindest acts of the wicked are cruel.
-Proverbs 12:10 NIV

"In the Talmud, there is a prohibition against owning a dangerous animal. Of course not all dogs are dangerous, but the halacha (law) is pretty clear that it's prohibited to own a dangerous one. The halacha, goes one step further, though. It is prohibited to own an animal that could be perceived as dangerous, even if it's not actually dangerous, because there is a certain damage that the fear of the animal could cause others and Torah living is very concerned with how one person's actions affect another's. The Talmud gives over a story of a pregnant woman who's petrified of a barking dog she passes on the street. The owner assures her that the bark is worse than the bite, but the woman informs him that she has already miscarried due to her immense fear." -Allison Josephs

I'm sure someone will object to me quoting a Jewish author who references the Talmud (widely trusted and highly respected historic rabbis commenting and expanding upon the Mishnah) but I think it's important to gleam what as much as possible from a variety of source material. No, I don't advocate living under Old Covenant laws. It's a fascinating quote that applies to our discussion, OK?

What happens when good dogs become violent? Long before I worked at a pet store I read *The Dog Whisperer* by Cesar Millan. I was fascinated by his TV show but I don't have cable so I'd watch a few episodes here and there online.

His results were beyond impressive. It was a hit because most TV viewers never imagined this level of success was possible with problematic dogs.

When I mentioned this book to the dog trainers at work, they made a big show of disliking Cesar and his methods. After a few brief conversations, it was clear that his methods weren't politically correct. His success was viewed as an affront to leading animal behavior experts with Ph.D.'s and other advanced degrees. It all sounded hypocritical to me because the trainers at my store wouldn't go near the kind of aggressive dogs that led to Cesar's success.

My co-workers would reluctantly acknowledge that his methods worked, but in the same breath, they would try to explain why their approach was vastly superior in every way, even if it didn't produce the same results. Cesar Milan trained dogs for celebrities, sure, but that was not the only reason for his success. Apart from his TV show, Cesar worked with a lot of "last chance" aggressive dogs on death row. He was their last hope before doggy death camp, and that's admirable.

When it comes to training dangerous dogs that no one else wants to touch, his skills remain unimpeachable to this day, but the haters are still hurling insults. He isn't perfect, but any honest trainer will admit that his common sense techniques work. I listened to my fellow trainer's opinions, but their alternatives to Cesar's approach left a lot to be desired. Most aggressive animal owners have treated their dogs harshly, (read: abuse) and prefer to chain up their dogs in the backyard (read: neglect).

As we learned in the previous chapter, abuse and neglect lead to disastrous results. Innocent dogs become a menace to their community and gnashing their teeth when anyone or anything approaches their territory. My fellow trainers had no reliable alternative to Cesar's brand of tough love, and only a fool would blindly trust a philosophy that cannot solve the most urgent problem in the industry.

The politically correct insanity reached its peak with our rabid animal, rapid response kit at work. This would have been hilarious if it was only a joke. After a few weeks on the job, I asked a co-worker about our absurd first aid kit. He showed me the emergency kit that was stashed at strategic locations around the store. It was reserved for dog attacks in our store. In the event of a violent outburst, this small plastic container was our first and only line of defense.

Some legal genius from the home office installed these things in every store and I bet it was costly to implement. Each one contained amazing, life-saving devices like a silent dog whistle and a little bottle of citronella based pepper spray. It's only reasonable to assume that one might hesitate before spraying a large, violent animal with mildly irritating essential oils, but that, in a nutshell, was our first and only line of defense.

The infamous box under each cash register earned its nickname; we called it the "*Mr. Roger's Neighborhood* riot kit." It was the butt of a few jokes but we all knew it couldn't help if a bull-mastiff latched onto the throat of your five-year-old son. What do you think? Personally, I would prefer a snub-nosed .357 revolver if a massive Cane Corso attacked a human in front of me. Can you imagine trying to save a child with a glorified squirt gun and a plastic dog whistle? Thankfully, we never had to use our corporate approved safety kit during my brief tenure at the big-box pet store.

All jokes aside, thousands of dog owners face legal trouble every year when their beloved animals turn violent. Whenever I see news stories about a dog that mutilated a person, the dog owner always looks dumbfounded as they stand there in court. A few of them should win Academy Awards for their dramatic portrayals of shock and denial. Guess who isn't surprised by the attack? Everyone else in his or her neighborhood.

Anyone with half a brain saw it coming a mile away and a few people probably tried to warn the owner. Did they listen? No, instead they deflected and rebuffed the concerns of reasonable, rational members of the community. Years of jail time and civil lawsuits could ruin your retirement plans and even force a wealthy family into bankruptcy proceedings. Please remember, this line of logic can be applied to any type of idolatry. When we're talking about dogs and idols, it's like a case study. The lessons here are useful for your situation, even if you're facing an entirely different temptation.

"Dog attacks account for over one-third of all homeowners insurance claims filed every year. Many end in lawsuits seeking damages." -injuryclaimcoach.com

"There are at least 4.7 million dog bites every year in the United States, based on figures that are more than 20 years old and which certainly must have grown since then..." - dogbitelaw.com

Let's consider the profile of a person who can turn ordinary dogs into violent monsters. This is more than just an angry guy with zero respect for leash laws and a disdain for fellow humans. This isn't just a sanctimonious jerk who refuses to pick up his dog's poop in your front yard. We're talking about adults who leave short-haired mammals chained to a concrete slab during the bitter cold winter.

Their dogs are miserable, so they bark all night, which drives everyone in the neighborhood crazy. In nature, dogs are free to seek shelter and dig holes. They share body heat with the other dogs in their pack and live in a climate that's suitable for their breed. Only a sociopath would treat a dog as if it were a machine.

This is the kind of person who might pay to watch a dog fight. On the surface, they appear to be cold or passive, but God only knows what they're thinking. I've seen my fair share of hundred-pound dogs that were barely under control.

You might envision a wild junkyard dog on the outskirts of town, but I've seen soccer moms pulled to the ground by large, overpriced guard dogs. It's not just the worst offenders and extreme examples that lead to death. There's a full spectrum of inhumane behavior and bad attitudes that lead to tragic results.

My wife and I have always enjoyed taking long walks together. When we were newlyweds we lived in a somewhat sketchy neighborhood near downtown San Antonio. After observing the unusual habits of our neighbors who all carried walking sticks, we took the hint and began to carry a walking stick to ward off stray dogs. It was a real nuisance, and in all my travels I've never seen anything like it. Most of them were harmless, but a few would run up to us growling and barking aggressively.

Even today, in a significantly nicer neighborhood, we cross the street to avoid unleashed dogs. When you have two toddlers, it's not worth the risk, and it's OK if that offends someone who breaks the law to suit their mood. Let's be clear, I don't know anything about you (besides the fact that you're brazenly defying the law in public). Has a dog ever tried to attack you or your kids? It's happened to me more than once and that's why I appreciate leash laws. If you're a stand-up guy or gal then prove it by obeying the law.

How is anyone supposed to know if your dog is safe or not? Oh yeah, that's right, because you see the frightened look on someone's face and then shout "it's OK, he's a nice dog!" Well, I guess that settles the matter. Let's call the mayor and ask for a special exemption badge. Everyone wants to be an exception to the rule. For future reference, there's no need to loudly announce your excuses to everyone who isn't visibly excited to see you. We're both on the same narrow hiking trail so I'm stuck with whatever happens.

In a situation like this, all we know is that you're brazenly violating a reasonable law, and in this context, you expect everyone to blindly trust you without question? The bizarre justification of a selfish person falls apart when you take a few minutes to unpack the issue and ask a few questions. Therefore, the only considerate choice is to esteem or value others above yourself. (Philippians 2:3)

That's still true even when it's inconvenient or unpleasant. Seriously, you don't know how your decisions make other people feel, and yes, that matters. Your choice to ignore leash laws is guaranteed to terrify people with PTSD from prior dog attacks. The fear of dogs, also known as Cynophobia, can be devastating. It's a common struggle for women, minorities, or anyone from the region of the world that's known as 10/40 window.

"The 10/40 Window is the rectangular area of North Africa, the Middle East and Asia approximately between 10 degrees north and 40 degrees north latitude. The 10/40 Window is often called "The Resistant Belt" and includes the majority of the world's Muslims, Hindus, and Buddhists." - Joshuaproject.net

With around 5 billion souls, the 10/40 window is home to the largest unreached people groups in the world. The Bible calls us to love strangers and foreigners (Zechariah 7:10) but that's impossible when we're stuck on ourselves. We have been sent into this world as ambassadors for Christ, and Jesus was extraordinarily selfless.

This may come as a surprise, but when you're walking down the street, total strangers don't owe you anything. Real Christians love their neighbor, so they make an effort to be kind and considerate. The Lord watches over the foreigner. (Psalm 146:9) The Bible tells us to love foreigners (Deuteronomy 10:19), to show them hospitality, (Hebrews 13:2) and do them no harm. (Matthew 25:35)

With all that sad, please take time to consider this verse before your next free-range jaunt in the park "the wisdom from above is first pure, then peaceable, gentle, reasonable, full of mercy and good fruits, unwavering, without hypocrisy. And the seed whose fruit is righteousness is sown in peace by those who make peace." -James 3:17,18 NASB

Instead of presuming upon others for the sake of your dog's freedom, it's better to remember Christ's call to be peacemakers (Matthew 5:9) who submit to one another out of reverence (Ephesians 5:21) and obey the laws of the land. (Romans 13:1) There's always a temptation to become overly confident to the point of presumptive arrogance, but please understand that such a bad attitude greatly diminishes our Christian witness. In other words, you'll make the rest of us look bad even if your dog is well behaved.

Chapter 11

Junkyard Dogs

"Put to death therefore what is earthly in you: sexual immorality, impurity, passion, evil desire, and covetousness, which is idolatry. On account of these the wrath of God is coming." -Colossians 3:5-6 ESV

"Colossians 3 is the key chapter that speaks to this issue. Verse 5 notes, "Put to death therefore what is earthly in you: sexual immorality, impurity, passion, evil desire, and covetousness, which is idolatry." Contrasting the former lives of his readers with their new life in Christ, Paul lists various sins that serve as other "gods" in place of Jesus Christ. He adds in verses 7–8, "In these you too once walked, when you were living in them. But now you must put them all away: anger, wrath, malice, slander, and obscene talk from your mouth." -CompellingTruth.org

How far would you go to defend an idol? Is any price too high? Prisons and jails are full of young adults who didn't realize how low they were willing to stoop until it was too late. All excuses aside, the sharpest moments of testing reveals our true character. God tests everything with fire, and that includes you on your worst day. We would like to be judged by our best days, but the real progress of maturity surfaces during challenges and conflicts. "Simon, Simon, behold, Satan has demanded permission to sift you like wheat". -Luke 22:31 NASB

Simon Peter failed the test on the night Jesus was betrayed and Jesus restored him shortly thereafter. The Lord is willing to restore you right now. When we repent and surrender our lives to the Lord, that single decision unleashes a rebuilding process with a good deal of personal reflection. A major benefit of rejecting idolatry is that it frees up your time. This is absolutely necessary, without lots of quiet time you can't process your thoughts or hear the still, small voice of God.

The most violent sinner can be transformed into a powerful champion, like the Apostle Paul. Being born again is exactly what it sounds like, a fresh start. It's the miracles of resurrection, and the same power that conquered the grave lives in you. Ice-cold atheists become red hot and full of zeal after experiencing the love of Jesus. Raging alcoholics find the strength to become sober and most will remain sober for the rest of their life. All around the world, the Holy Spirit is successfully restoring families and rebuild communities through conviction, and a Godly sorry that leads to repentance. (2 Corinthians 7:10)

God gets the glory when we declare "I will never be the same again", but at some point, many of us drift back into the same old sins. There are only two paths, one leads to eternal life, the other is the broad road to destruction. When idolatry flares up in our daily life, we have a choice to reject it or to be the fool who "gives full vent to his rage" (Proverbs 29:11). Those who cannot control their temper are never more than one bad decision away from bloodshed.

If you've ever wanted to fight someone over a parking space or an important project at work, that's the spirit of murder. Anger is the early stage, but without restraint, it always leads to a manifestation of violence. As we know, fantasizing about violence is as bad as murder itself. (Matthew 5:22) You might not personally feel tempted by outbursts of anger, but we all feel the effects of unbridled anger in one way or another.

I was thinking about this on the day I earned my dog training certificate. It was also the day I discovered our store's policy on aggressive breeds. If the animal in question looked like a fighting breed or a guard dog, they were not allowed to attend group or private training classes. Basically, they didn't allow scary-looking dogs inside the store.

I didn't like the rule at first, but they had a very clear business model. Years later, after having kids of my own, I can see it from a different point of view. Situations like this are a bit of a conundrum since you're stuck between a rock and a hard place. After all, those big, abused, and neglected animals did need help. I don't resent their decision to play it safe, but it caused me to reflect on Christians who've been rejected by a local church. Please allow me to explain.

What would you think if a couple of big, rough-looking bikers wandered into your church? They might be ex-cons or former gang members. In general, church folk have a certain look and feel that's easily recognizable to outsiders. I know there are exceptions, but let's be honest, there's often a high degree of conformity in most denominations. If you don't wear khakis and polos, you might feel awkward at first.

Did you know some folks won't go to church because they don't have dress clothes? Maybe they've been kicked out of a church when they were younger or come from a poor family. Whatever the case may be, they don't know all the unspoken rules (and there are plenty of unspoken rules at most churches).

You could take them out shopping and buy them a couple of dress shirts, slacks, and a pair of shoes. A new outfit and a haircut would cost less than $100. If that's too much money, take them to a thrift shop and you'll spend less than $20. Pastors might preach about being seeker-friendly, but it takes a village to make it happen. I've visited hundreds of churches of various denominations, and most were more similar than different.

Most of the people I've met have been very polite, but it's hard to get past the small talk when church feels like a spectator sport, and I'm in the audience, watching a performance. I can make friends anywhere, so if I have a hard time connecting, then I can only imagine what it's like for someone with a rough background. When we fail to find deep, meaningful relationships, we're liable to give up and stop trying.

When any local church allows vulnerable people to slip through the cracks, it means the congregation has become nearsighted and cliquish. There are dozens of ways to exclude someone without overtly telling them to go away. Even the biggest bully has a heart, he feels the sting of being a social outcast. It's not unreasonable to suggest that a large number of mass shootings could be prevented by a few good friends who take the time to befriend a troubled soul. Is that a good enough reason to lay down your idols?

If someone dressed like a gang-banger walked into your church, how would you respond? Maybe introduce yourself and start a friendly conversation, or would you avoid eye contact and talk to someone you already know? Mass shootings in churches have become common, which is why we must be sharp, shrewd and alert. You might think it's wrong for leaders and greeters to use behavioral recognition or criminal profiling strategies, but few would disagree if I said everyone should treat the church building as if it were their home. That means you stand up, walk over and greet each new guest without hesitation.

Good, old fashioned kindness is a solution to unseen problems. The spiritual gift of hospitality just feels nice, (yes, this applies to introverts too). It can be emotionally disarming in certain circumstances, but in a worst case scenario, your presence will help you prevent or reduce the harm that may be caused by a violent criminal. Problems like this are best handled up close and personal. Don't be the guy who ignores visitors at church, that's one of the main reasons visitors don't feel welcomed.

Churches are packed with a high percentage of "cultural Christians" who enjoy the social aspects of church but aren't interested in living for Christ. If we aren't laboring in the Great Harvest, it's only ever the result of unbelief. No matter what is preached from the pulpit, cultural Christians fail to connect the dots between faith and deeds, or "the kindness and severity of God" (James 2:26, Romans 11:22,

John 4:24). If we learned to fear the Lord we would not fear humans.

It's time to worship in "spirit and truth" and I like to think of this as the best of both worlds. It's the best traits of old fashioned, traditional churches and the new breed of young, charismatic, Spirit-filled churches. Real unity starts with re-uniting generations as much as denominations. The spirit of division is made worst by the spirit of control. Unity in freedom is the opposite of the demonic spirit of control. Unity is a full agreement with the written word without quenching the manifestations of the Holy Spirit.

As the worldwide church grows in unity, we can expect to see greater victories among the most aggressive people. Judging by outward appearances is just as wrong as judging someone by the church they attend. The trend is changing, thanks in part to the increased availability of safe, low cost travel and free educational resources online. (Daniel 12:4) Bad theology is still widespread, but it has been lessened significantly among legitimate believers.

Most of us grew up in church, and that's great, but being a "lifer" comes with a unique set of blind spots and challenges. Lifelong Christians often fail to understand the perspective of those who grew up outside of Christianity. We often have a habit of clinging to comfort, safety and familiar social cliques without leaving room for evangelism or church visitors. However, if you outsource all that work, you'll miss most of what God wants to develop inside you. One body many parts, that's true, but there's no mystery regarding the fact that hardly anyone 'feels led' to clean church toilets or visit the local retirement community.

A great multitude of believers are eager to preach and sing on stage, but only a precious few faithfully show up to prayer meetings. Every one of us is called to direct evangelism and charity, but most of us are content with dropping a few bucks in the offering plate. A sailboat is safest in the harbor, but ships were built to sail in open water.

Making an idol of safety and comfort is the opposite of what Jesus demonstrated by laying down His life. The righteous are bold as a lion, if you lack boldness, even after praying for it, you might want to reevaluate your commitment to purity.

Are you willing to accept the risk that's associated with serving orphans, foreigners, and ex-cons? If we live in fear and refuse to help the least of these, how can we expect to have any inheritance in Christ? Personal sacrifices must be made for the sake of spiritual warfare.

I hope you will choose to share your faith with rough characters who hang out in dangerous places. I sincerely doubt that Jesus met all those publicans and prostitutes in a synagogue! Don't forfeit another battle that could be won by you showing up and taking a stand. Too much ground has been lost due to negligence on our part, so give it your best shot and trust God for the increase. God carefully places people in your life, so engage in a warm, friendly two-way conversation and "earnestly contend for the faith". -Jude 1:3 KJV

Don't give up on the aggressive humans in your life unless the Holy Spirit closes a door, or leads you to focus on someone else. Find an open ear even if it's attached to someone who looks terrifying. Don't worry if you get a bloody nose or a bruised knee once in a while, love endures all things. "Behold, I send you out as sheep in the midst of wolves; so be shrewd as serpents and innocent as doves." - Matthew 10:16 NASB

Working with troublemakers will leave you sharp and strong, but constantly avoiding trouble makes you dull, weak and shallow. When you're in a tight situation it forces you to be more alert and vigilant. It's your choice to view life as an exciting adventure. It's your choice to stand between the living and the dead like Moses and Aaron. (Numbers 16:48)

God has a specific assignment that includes a unique set of gifts that are yours alone. The times are growing darker, suicide rates are at an all-time high, over a hundred thousand people die each day, and no one is promised another day. Don't give up on anyone who makes an honest effort. Love your brother no matter how many times they stumble and fall. Cultural Christians love to shoot their wounded.

So beware of spiritual rabies, which is a fault-finding spirit that's almost as contagious as it is destructive. Beloved, there's no such thing as a gift of criticism, please don't volunteer to be Satan's volunteer prosecutor. It won't end well. The devil's title is The Accuser of the Brethren, and I guarantee you don't want his lot in life or the afterlife. It won't be much better for those who do his dirty work. "...for whom the gloom of utter darkness has been reserved forever... These are grumblers, malcontents, following their own sinful desires; they are loud-mouthed boasters, showing favoritism to gain advantage." -Jude 1:13-16

Love alone must motivate us to restore one another gently, without doing the work of the accuser. "But even the archangel Michael, when he was disputing with the devil about the body of Moses, did not himself dare to condemn him for slander but said, "The Lord rebuke you!"" -Jude 1:9 NIV

Whenever we lash out against someone we understand or make harsh demands from others, we are not walking in love. "Brothers, if anyone is caught in any transgression, you who are spiritual should restore him in a spirit of gentleness. Keep watch on yourself, lest you too be tempted." -Galatians 6:1 ESV

Learn to love the aggressive humans in life. God our Father loves "the least of these" just as much as He loves Jesus. Yes, He loves us with the same intensity as Jesus. Love will lead you to do more than you could ever imagine. Let's love everyone that God puts in our life, and cheerfully carry their burdens for a few miles. (Matthew 5:41)

Proverbs says "Where there are no oxen, the manger is clean, but abundant crops come by the strength of the ox."

-Proverbs 14:1 ESV That little nugget of wisdom isn't only about livestock. The "oxen" in your life are the "pit-bull" people who have never felt welcome in church. Behold, Jesus stands at the door and knocks, I bet He does this dressed like a homeless person, will you welcome The Lord by loving the least of these?

With your help, even the roughest characters will grow up to be mighty men and women of valor. They have been forgiven much and will love much. (Luke 7:47) Their courage will be legendary and your fearless obedience is a critical step in the process. Will you serve the retired soldiers and sailor-mouthed sheepdogs, even after they ruffle your feathers for the millionth time? Or, will you defend the easily offended old fogies who donate the most money?

At the end of the day it's your choice; to be a father to the fatherless, and live by faith, or treat church like a business. Whatever you do, I hope you will make time for the messy humans in your life. It will be nice to have those "junkyard dogs" on your side when the going gets tough. "From the days of John the Baptist until now the kingdom of heaven suffers violence, and violent men take it by force." - Matthew 11:12 NASB

Anything I put before my God is an idol
Anything I want with all my heart is an idol
Anything I can't stop thinking of is an idol
Anything that I give all my love is an idol
'Cause I can sing all I want to
And still get it wrong
Worship is more than a song
Clear the stage and set the sound and lights ablaze
If that's the measure you must take to crush the idols

-Jimmy Needham

Chapter 12

Pet obsessions

"but the poor man had nothing except one little ewe lamb he had bought. He raised it, and it grew up with him and his children. It shared his food, drank from his cup and even slept in his arms. It was like a daughter to him." -2 Samuel 12:3 NIV

"When Leona Helmsley, known as the "Queen of Mean", died in 2007 she left $12 million to her Maltese, Trouble. Fortune magazine branded it the third dumbest business moment of 2007... Carl Lekic, the general manager of one of Helmsley's hotels, looked after Trouble, receiving $60,000 a year for his troubles. Another $8,000 went for grooming, $1,200 for food and $100,000 went for full-time security, as Trouble had received numerous death threats." -Justin Nobel

Have you ever met a kooky cat lady? We've all heard jokes about an eccentric old man or woman who lives with fifteen feline roommates and wears cat-themed clothing, but if you take the time to befriend them, you will quickly realize it's no laughing matter. Animal hoarding is becoming an epidemic that leads to disastrous results and police intervention. Most house pets can multiply quickly because they have large litters, and it's hard to find a suitable home for everyone.

The so-called experts who preach against euthanasia are like Pharisees. They won't lift a finger to carry the heavy burden they lay upon others. (Luke 11:46) There's a big difference between a well funded, fully staffed animal shelter and a private residence that's run into the ground by someone who isn't making the best choices in the first place.

An animal hoarder is almost always an isolated individual who shifts his affections to animals after rejecting close relationships with humans. It's the portrait of a cold (or deeply confused) heart that's lost in fantasyland. The lonely animal hoarder feels accepted, loved, and important because the animals depend on her. She often develops a delusional messiah complex which further complicates the matter. When someone falsely believes that animal lives are equal to humans, she will do whatever it takes to care for as many animals as possible. God's commandments protect us from all kinds of unnecessary suffering.

I once read an article about a lonely old woman who died at home. She was a crazy cat lady with twenty or thirty cats in a small apartment. Long forgotten by friends and family, no one noticed her absence or bothered to pay a visit. Years turned into decades and somewhere along the way, cats became the center of her universe.

Eventually, her neighbors called the police after noticing a bad smell and a growing pile of newspapers by her front door. The newspapers say she died from natural causes, but what happened next was straight out of a scary movie. After a few days, those darn cats turned her corpse into a dinner buffet. How's that for unconditional love? Her furry roommates feasted on her flesh for weeks, and the very thought of it brings me great grief. Beloved, this is a sign of the times.

Your life is probably a far cry from this extreme case, but if pet-related spending consumes a large portion of your disposable income, then it's time to rethink your priorities. When the hours, minutes and dollars are added up, animal expenditures should never outweigh your ministry contributions. I'd say the same thing to anyone whose crazy about Christmas decorations or designer handbags. "But if anyone does not provide for his relatives, and especially for members of his household, he has denied the faith and is worse than an unbeliever." -1 Timothy 5:8 ESV

Jesus is talking about your family in this verse, but Jesus also said the church is your real family, just as much as anyone else. "who is my mother and brother?" (citation) The story of that woman's death was tragic, and I'm sure the same could be said about her life's story. There's no easy answer to extreme situations like this, but a strong local community is a big part of the solution. To treat animals better than people requires a flat out rejection of the greatest commandment to love God and neighbors. Jesus said all of the law and the prophets hang on love, but anyone who claims to love God alone (and not their neighbor) is like a college student who earns a 50% grade on a big test. When it comes to love, getting it half right is a flat out failure.

The same is true for Christians who trust the Lord for their salvation, but fail to run with most of what Jesus taught. Legitimate love for God always leads to love for humans. Even a high school dropout knows that answering only half the questions correctly on an exam will result in a failing grade. Even if you answer around 60% correct, that's a failing grade in most places.

In the business world, everyone from doctors and accountants to lawyers and mortgage professionals are required to complete annual continuing education courses. Nearly all of these tests require a score of 85% or higher if you want to acquire or retain professional credentials. Believers should study the Bible regularly, even if they graduated with honors from a prestigious Bible college or seminary. There's just too much at stake to feel confident with something you studied ten or twenty years ago.

God tests everyone, (1 Peter 1:6,7) but those who stubbornly cling to idols have no reason to expect God's blessings right now or treasures in Heaven. As we learned in chapter 2, John the Beloved took it a step further when he said; "If someone says, "I love God," and hates his brother, he is a liar; for the one who does not love his brother whom he has seen, cannot love God whom he has not seen." -1 John 4:20 NASB

Those who reject the Lord promote statements like this; "If it makes you happy, it can't be that bad," but for a logical point of view, that's demonstrably false. Don't take my word for it, all it takes is one visit to a jail or prison. If you have the courage, go and volunteer with a prison ministry, then you can have a conversation with a convicted murderer or rapist. Ask them, and most will admit that their crimes made them happy (in the heat of the moment) and it really was that bad.

Others will say you can do whatever you want as long as you don't harm others, but that also fails the logic test. We are never fully aware of the effects of our decisions. There are plenty of men and women who derive pleasure from abusing others. Whatever they're doing may or may not be legal, but that doesn't always determine right from wrong. Even the smallest acts of selfishness cause a ripple effect that cannot be fully understood or measured in this age.

Mature Christians know that "following your heart" is dangerous because feeling are not facts. We are called to step out in faith first. If you can always see the other side then it wouldn't be faith at all. Resist the urge to "walk by sight" because when you escape from being stuck in idolatry after years of dullness, it's impossible to gauge how blind you've become.

We are free to make choices, but we are not free from the consequences of those choices. Following your heart sounds wonderful, but isn't that exactly what King David did when he kidnapped Bathsheba and killed her husband? Idols come in every shape and size, but Jesus won't share you with another lover. Spiritual prostitution is what we do when we seek fulfillment in the arms of an idol. I'd recommend reading Hosea if you're unfamiliar with the concept of spiritual unfaithfulness.

God wants to help you avoid trouble, but at the same time, God will not be mocked. Consider this; the Old and New Testament are full of "cause and effect" stories with "if-then" scenarios. For example; if you do good, then God will bless you. If you persist in doing evil, then you will suffer the natural and spiritual consequences. Every book in the Bible recounts stories with a central them of what happens as a direct result of actions like obedience, disobedience, generosity, and stubbornness.

We will answer for every word and action, and since God is impartial, we know that feelings are not the litmus test of right and wrong. Sin is pleasurable for a season, (Hebrews 11:25) but in the long run, it produces a bitter fruit of thorns and thistles. "If anyone, then, knows the good they ought to do and doesn't do it, it is sin for them." -James 4:17 NIV

Beloved, we cannot fail the personal integrity test because no one has an excuse that carries weight in the eternal scales of justice and righteousness. Jesus is fully God but He is fully man. He's been there, He can empathize and sympathize with your situation. Nobody's perfect, sure, but how many times have we used that line as an excuse? Instead, we should use this amazing grace as a motivation to press on towards the goal of being perfected in Christ. (Hebrews 10:14, Matthew 5:48, 1 John 4:12, Philippians 3:12-15)

I listed several verses because the pursuit of perfection has been rejected by millions of nominal believers. They are the cultural Christians who don't think it's necessary to run with diligence or aim for perfection. They call that legalism. "Jesus replied, "You are in error because you do not know the Scriptures or the power of God." -Matthew 22:29 NIV

Nominal Christians rarely read anything from the New Testament, so the Old Testament doesn't stand a chance. Their favorite verse is "judge not lest ye be judged" but the context is always ignored. Jesus was speaking against condemnation and hypocrisy, not sound judgment. Discernment is good and it's necessary for safe and sound decision-making. (Proverbs 3:21 8:14)

If using sound judgment was sinful, then Jesus would not teach us how to judge (John 7:24) and there wouldn't be a book in the Bible called Judges. Moses was human just like us, and he had to judge all kinds of serious situations. Furthermore, you cannot say judging is wrong without making a judgment that it's wrong to judge. Isn't it ironic? All of your decision making requires some form of judment. If someone steals your car, you want the judge to rule in your favor, and return the car.

The Bible didn't contradict itself when it taught us how to judge. Instead, we should view the phrase "judge not" as a dichotomy. Here's another example. "Do not answer a fool according to his folly, or you yourself will be just like him. Answer a fool according to his folly, or he will be wise in his own eyes." -Proverbs 26:4,5 NIV

Which one is it, should I answer the fool or not? This is like being stuck between a rock and a hard place. There may not be an easy solution, so you'll have to judge if speaking up is worth the potential fallout. Judgment is a double edged sword, so it cuts both ways.

Instead of judging harshly or being rash, it's prudent to forgive and show mercy. If you aren't mature enough to extend grace for the sake of love, then at least do it for the sake of self preservation. "For in the way you judge, you will be judged; and by your standard of measure, it will be measured to you." -Matthew 7:2 NASB

In context, the phrase "do not judge" is better

understood like this; Condemn not, lest ye be condemned. Don't condemn your neighbor, and don't believe the lie that says your sins are minor but mine are major. Be gracious, especially with your brothers and sisters in Christ because "there is now no condemnation for those who are in Christ Jesus..." (Romans 8:1)

If we're being honest, when people say "don't judge me" what they mean to say is "don't you dare question my sinful lifestyle". They honor God with their lips, but their hearts are far from Him. (Isaiah 29:13, Matthew 15:8) Tough love is the antidote, and that's the kind of real love that leads you to confront friends, family, and neighbors on occasion.

You have the objectivity that they lack and vice versa. So how do we make righteous judgments without being a hypocrite? Start by walking in purity and read the Bible daily. Take the plank out of your eye. Why? So you can help others with the speck in their eye. (citation) Read what it says, then do what it says. If you only receive the word from sermons on YouTube, you're missing out on most of what God is saying.

"Pay attention to what you hear: with the measure you use, it will be measured to you, and still more will be added to you. For to the one who has, more will be given, and from the one who has not, even what he has will be taken away." -Mark 4:25 ESV

Hundreds of millions of humans face the constant threat of starvation and they are immeasurably more important than house pets. Billions face the daily crisis of spiritual starvation. In America, the poorest people are often obese. Similarly, most spiritually deficient Christians are spiritual gluttons who have never connected the dots between hearing and doing. They're "always learning but never able to come to a knowledge of the truth." 2 Timothy 3:7 NIV

It's easy to smile at church and keep the conversation

light, but that's only reasonable when that certain someone doesn't need help. Our sweet cat lady from the beginning of this chapter probably faced a similar struggle many times before giving up on humans. Was anyone willing to be a true friend who would invest significant time into that relationship?

It's easy to hide behind polite, superficial conversations. I bet she cried out for help on many occasions. Like the story of The Good Samaritan, most of us simply look the other way and avoid anyone who might be in trouble. Tough love doesn't just walk away without making an honest effort to intervene. When the time comes, a real friend will sound the alarm, even when it's met with anger and denial. "Iron sharpens iron, So one man sharpens another." -Proverbs 27:17 NASB

Tough love is the choice to lay down less important tasks and help someone whose struggling. People are more important than our most ambitious projects. Tough love can be costly, but it's a real game changer. It's the best strategy for a long-lasting breakthrough, but it only works when you clean up your act.

The point is mutual edification, to remove everything that hinders. "Judge not" isn't about turning a blind eye to sin, it's about working towards holiness together. We are far from perfect and yet we are being perfected through Christ. God alone is good, but when we get to Heaven all anyone wants to hear is, "Well done, thou good and faithful servant" -Matthew 25:21 KJV

Stumbling occasionally is a world apart from being slaves to sin. I am no longer a slave to sin. Sinners make a detailed plan to sin. Unrepentant sinners move their schedules around to accommodate their favorite sin. They save up money for their idols and go into debt to buy bigger, fancier idols. They waste countless hours daydreaming about debauchery. They drink slop from a pig's trough when there's a perfectly clean, crystal clear wellspring a few feet away.

Stumbling and failing (what we all do) is not the same as living in agreement with sin. We must be clear about this point to avoid deception. There's no neutral territory on this bloody battlefield. There's no fence to straddle, you can't travel to Switzerland and make a peace treaty with the devil. He will destroy your loved ones if possible, so what are you going to do about it?

We have been thrust into a spiritual war, which means serious injuries and casualties are an everyday occurrence. There's no neutral ground, not one inch. Your adversary the devil is working overtime, and that's still true even if you don't believe in demons or hell.

Forget what the TV says, go straight to the source and invest more time into the Bible. Your eternal rewards will not be determined by your wealth, academic achievements or superior theology. It's simple things like brotherly love, personal purity, discipleship, and perseverance. Remember, you're only a 'work in progress' if you keep working!

Mistakes are a normal part of a Pilgrim's Progress, and honest mistakes don't make you a hypocrite. Jesus isn't surprised by your failures, He loves you during your weakest attempts to follow Him. "Are not two sparrows sold for a penny? Yet not one of them will fall to the ground outside your Father's care. And even the very hairs of your head are all numbered. So don't be afraid; you are worth more than many sparrows." -Matthew 10:29-31 NIV

Chapter 13

Vitamins for Dogs, or
Supplements for a lonely heart?

"Calling me a "pet parent," and even worse, calling dog training "pet parenting," may be questionable in any number of ways, but above all, it lacks authenticity. "Pet parent" is the language of the marketer, of the ad campaign designed to sell you pet food and drugs and services by implying that doing "less" for your pets than your children means you don't really love them." -Christie Keith

"Like a dog that returns to its vomit is a fool who repeats his folly." -Proverbs 26:11 ESV

It's easy to stop by the pet store after work and grab a few items without considering all the recent changes in this rapidly growing industry. The pet product market has experienced explosive, exponential growth over the past twenty years. Americans spent around 63 billion dollars on their pets in 2017 alone. The great recession that began in 2008 couldn't stop the trend, but what we see today is a world apart from the friendly, neighborhood pet shops from my childhood.

As a new dog trainer, my perspective changed when I spent forty hours per week, in the belly of the beast. Part of my job involved memorizing the layout of the store, and keeping up with new products. Our customers looked up to trainers as experts, and they asked for our recommendations on nearly everything. I often helped customers compare product labels and helped straighten the shelves in the mornings when the store was slow.

The issue of dogs as it relates to idolatry occurred to me after meeting a nutritional supplement sales rep who specialized in pet products. Our company brought him in to educate our staff after installing a large vitamin and supplement display case. The large, beautiful case was place front and center. From the first day, every trainer knew it would be a cash cow. Fifty dollars for a bottle of doggy vitamins? I was absolutely flabbergasted.

That was my epiphany moment. Our economy was in shambles, but we had a constant stream of affluent, suburban customers lined up to buy organic doggy shampoo, hand-knitted holiday sweaters, grass-fed, refrigerated raw meat and beef jerky for dogs. I felt the Lord impress upon me, as clear as day, this was idolatry.

I must have read a hundred Christian books by this point, but I didn't understand idolatry. I don't remember hearing pastors teach about it at churches or conferences. They may have mentioned it briefly, but it was never emphasized, which is odd because it's a big deal in the Bible. So I went home after work and spent hours reading about idol worship from a wide variety of online resources. I searched through my favorite commentaries and concordances for passages that addressed idol worship.

My curiosity slowly turned into a multi-year study about the true cost of unfaithfulness. Over the years I've met countless pet owners who candidly admit to being obsessive. Each one of those conversations has inspired me to keep going and finish this book. I cannot tell you how many divine encounters and nudges from the Lord have been given to remind me that this is important.

When I was a little boy I remember the first time I walked into the new supermarket in my hometown of Lawrence Kansas. We marveled at the automatic doors, ice-cold air conditioning, and dizzying selection of food. It was massive compared to other grocery stores back then. Even so, supermarkets from the 1980s carried a small selection of animal products by today's standards. My hometown supermarket had one half of one side of one aisle dedicated to pet products. Now it's common to see several aisles set aside for pet products in supermarkets, general stores, and discount stores.

Pet shops from thirty years ago were tiny and quaint compared to the massive warehouse stores that dominate the industry today. From a business perspective, it's only logical that publicly traded companies would pursue growth to capture as much market share as possible. I can't blame the world for being worldly, that's normal.

"What agreement is there between the temple of God and idols? For we are the temple of the living God. As God has said: "I will live with them and walk among them, and I will be their God, and they will be my people." Therefore, "Come out from them and be separate, says the Lord. Touch no unclean thing, and I will receive you."" -2 Corinthians 6:17 NIV

Real Christians are a peculiar people. Our citizenship is not of this world and Jesus said the world would hate us because we are being conformed into His image. (John 15:18, Romans 8:29) Therefore come out and be separate. That's a hard pill to swallow because it means exactly what it says. We have been set apart (made holy) by Christ Himself. It's our job to remain holy, to keep ourselves clean, even in the worst circumstance. How can we keep our feet clean in this world? It's impossible without the Holy Spirit, but what we have in Christ Jesus is more than enough.

To the world, idolatry is nothing more than splurging a little here and there. My parent's generation grew up watching shows like Lassie and The Adventures of Rin Tin Tin. We've come a long way since then. Now we can browse through dozens of dog and pet-centric shows on cable and streaming TV. If that isn't enough, you can pay extra to stream TV channels specifically designed for dogs to watch while you're away from home.

Americans are spending more on animals every year, even when their income stays the same. Pet expenditures increased through the great recession, despite the financial situation, and the market for premium pet food is rapidly growing. Companies were shutting down and struggling to stay afloat, as foreclosures were at an all time high. Blood was in the streets, as they say, but nonessential pet purchases continued to overtake more of our income compared to previous years.

Idolatry spreads like an aggressive cancer and it's never satisfied with second best. Just like any addiction, idolatry dominates your time and money, leaving only scraps for friends, family and the ministry. Online shopping makes it even easier to fritter away your time, money, and talents whenever you feel the urge. You can buy almost anything with the click of a button from the comfort of your living room.

Massive as they are, big-box pet stores can only carry a small fraction of what's available online through websites like Amazon and eBay. The parable of the wheat and weeds is actively unfolding right before our eyes. It's no wonder the mark of the beast revolves around commerce. As the end of the age approaches, people grow into the fullness of what they've decided to manifest. Over time, everyone grows closer to God the Father or the devil. (John 8:44)

I once worked with a guy who placed bets online at work. This was nearly twenty years ago when online gambling was in its infancy. He couldn't wait to waste his paycheck. So, instead of working on the job, my co-worker gambled with his salary while stealing time from our employer. That industry has exploded since then, it's grown to the point that ESPN regularly features gambling experts.

Two opposite harvests are slowly wrapping up within the church itself. What would you do if you realized that most of the warnings in the Bible were directed at the church, not the world? The devil has a long term strategy to keep you distracted with big problems and little trifles. When you fail to show up for battle, you lose by default. The enemy easily steers millions away from the great harvest with idolatry. Spiritual warfare is constantly ceded to the enemy by sleepy Christians who cling to worthless idols.

God didn't establish a bunch of rules to ruin our fun. He gave us brilliant, helpful New Covenant to make our lives better right now. It's the only battle plan that leads to victory. When our priorities are stuck on objects made from wood, metal, and plastic, our perspective becomes twisted and distorted. When we veer off track we invariably lead others astray.

Your dog isn't the problem. It's the fantasy world you've built up around that relationship that leads to a strong delusion. One of my fellow dog trainers told me a story about his wife that I'll never forget. For years she dreamed about owning a Yorkshire Terrier and coveted her friend's expensive little purse-puppies. My buddy was far from rich, but after years of begging and pleading, he relented.

With the help of a credit card, they went out and bought the dog of her dreams at a posh, overpriced puppy mill. A few days later his wife was at home with their four-year-old daughter who was happily playing by a large bay window in their living room. It had a great view of the backyard and the little girl adored her new puppy. She sat there watching it chase squirrels among the autumn leaves on a brisk, beautiful morning.

Without warning, a big hawk swooped down, snatched the puppy, and flew away. The little girl saw it happen and went ballistic. She was inconsolable for hours. Needless to say, it was a bad day for everyone at their house. As my co-worker so eloquently put it, at around two thousand dollars, this was the most expensive lunch he'd ever bought. A few weeks later, life settled down for the traumatized family, and they adopted a feisty, fifty-pound mutt from the local animal shelter.

The moral of the story;

1. Do not covet thy neighbor's doggy
2. Do not try to keep up with the Joneses

3. Do not leave a puppy outside alone in Kansas

Chapter 14

Chemo for Calicos

"Be sober-minded; be watchful. Your adversary the devil prowls around like a roaring lion, seeking someone to devour." -1 Peter 5:8 ESV

"Of the $1.05 trillion revenue for the global pharmaceutical market, nearly half of it -- roughly $515 billion -- comes from the U.S. and Canada. However, the two countries make up only around 7% of the total world population." -The Motley Fool

A few days ago I was leaving a restaurant and noticed a flyer on the wall for a missing French Bulldog. They offered a fifteen thousand dollar reward to anyone with information that led to the return of their beloved dog. I shouldn't be shocked by such a princely sum of money, especially considering what I've learned from writing this book, but it still took me by surprise.

A quick search online reveals insanely high figures offered (and paid) for missing house pets. What would you give to have your favorite pet returned if they were lost? Most of us aren't too worried about kitty kidnappers, but then again, trips to the Veterinarian can feel like a robbery at times.

That brings us to the issue of animal healthcare. This

is another touchy subject, and even if I could manage to perfectly speak the truth in love, it's impossible to avoid offense. How much would you spend to treat a sick or dying dog? It seems like every vet's office has an attractive display of financing options. Would you take out a loan for animal medical bills? Or, are you currently paying off debt from pet-related expenses?

We live in a beautiful world, but it's brutally unforgiving for humans who cannot afford a visit to the pharmacy or a doctor's care. It's even worse for someone who can't afford soap and toothpaste. Would you pay five or ten thousand dollars to provide chemotherapy for a cat with cancer?

Instead of honoring the Lord with our first fruits, God gets the scraps from our table like a dog. Don't take my word for it, take a few minutes to search online and read about how much (or how little rather) church members are giving in tithes and offerings. (10) Instead of helping the poor, we buy little luxuries for ourselves and our pets.

- Tithers make up only 10-25 percent of a normal congregation
- Only 5 percent of the U.S. Tithes, 80 percent of Americans give 2%
- Christians give 2.5% per capita, during the Great Depression they gave 3.3% -RelevantMagazine.com

How can anyone claim to love the poor when their pets receive better healthcare than most humans? A simple procedure at the vet, like feline tooth extractions, costs around $500. If your beloved Beagle eats a random object that won't pass, a gastronomical operation might be $2,000.

Those examples are emergencies that require urgent care, but not everything fits this category. Would you spend $140 per month on insulin for your Irish Setter? Over ten years that adds up to $16,800 or more depending on inflation.

Financial Planners often share the story of a young person who decides to invest one dollar each day. With a little diligence, $365 a year will most likely grow into a multimillion-dollar retirement account. Imagine how much treasure you could store up in Heaven by donating a dollar a day to God's harvest. The Bible instructs us to be prudent, and part of prudence is planning for the future. (Proverbs 1:4, 8:12)

Honestly, I'm not surprised when people become belligerent over the issue of generosity. We're discussing life-saving, cutting-edge medical treatments that most humans could never afford. Crippled people around the world would do anything for the kind of custom-made prosthetic limbs that house pets regularly receive in wealthy, Western nations.

The root of this issue is a lack of charity towards humans. When someone is uncharitable with their words while defending their choice to withhold charity from humans, at least they're being consistent with their belief system. It all goes back to the lie that says animals are equal to humans. Fair warning; if you speak out against idolatry, be prepared for resistance. Fanatic idolaters are eager to steal, kill, and destroy for their idols.

If you will consider what I'm saying, it all goes back to the same financial conundrum. Your time and money are limited, and my goal is to persuade believers to spend more on what Jesus emphasized, (charity for poor humans, widows, outcasts, etc.,) and less on everything else. Jesus rebuked the Pharisees and scribes for neglecting their family. They used their ministry as an excuse to abandon their family's needs. Judging by a plain reading of Matthew 15, we can see it's worse to withhold generosity from your family, and the ministry, all for the sake of animals.

"For God commanded, 'Honor your father and your mother,' and, 'Whoever reviles father or mother must surely die.' But you say, 'If anyone tells his father or his mother,

"What you would have gained from me is given to God," he need not honor his father.' So for the sake of your tradition you have made void the word of God." -Matthew 15:4-6 ESV

Experienced pet owners know that an emergency trip to the Vet could cost thousands of dollars. That's a huge pile of cash for most people. Where do you draw the line with medical treatments for animals? I think it's wise to have that discussion before an emergency strikes. If you can't afford the occasional, unexpected trip to the vet, then you shouldn't keep pets. Also, if you feel convicted about the high cost of responsible pet ownership, then it's time to reconsider your priorities in light of eternity.

What should you do when your pets die? Most of us don't live in a place where you can legally dig a hole in the backyard to bury a dog. Are you willing to pay for a doggy funeral or a cremation? During my research, I was surprised to find approximately one thousand animal funeral homes in America.

Final arrangements for a pet can be as expensive as you want them to be. There's no shortage of businesses that will free you from the burden of a healthy bank account. Funeral packages often include bouquets of fresh flowers, a beautiful casket, and burial plots with a personalized granite headstone. In case you're wondering, yes, that's expensive. Nevertheless, hundreds of thousands of dogs are lionized with funerals every year, and the trend is, you guessed it, growing steadily.

Society has drastically shifted on issues like this in a single generation. Self-absorbed consumerism has become my generation's version of the sexual revolution from the 1960s, and in my opinion, it's just another sign of the times.

Half a century ago, veterinarian work was generally limited to income-producing farm animals like sheep, cattle, and horses. It's important to take your pet to the doctor when they're sick or injured, but you are not morally obligated to pay for every procedure that's recommended. Sometimes, the most humane thing to do is put an older animal to sleep and end its suffering. I would never say that about humans because animals are not people.

Honoring God with your money doesn't always feel good, but it's a real lifesaver. A rancher relies on the Vet to protect the main source of his livelihood. Most of us cannot say the same. At a dairy farm, cows provide delicious food for the community and a primary source of income for dairy owners, employees and their families.

When I was young, spending thousands of dollars on a family dog was unthinkable. It wasn't a matter of having enough money, it was about priorities and propriety. I found an article recently about a crowdfunding campaign that raised $45,000 in donations for an Australian Collie that was hit by a snowplow. The medical bills were estimated at $10,000 for the dog. I began to wonder, would my story go viral if I was hit by a snowplow? It's not likely.

Thankfully I can rely on God to supply my every need. People often ask, why can't I do both? Well, that's between you and the Lord, but the research I've provided in this book would suggest that we don't do both, not very well. No one can serve two masters, and I'm suggesting that more Christians become radical about Christ and let someone else worry about breeding animals for pleasure and comfort.

I don't begrudge anyone for keeping pets, but thousands of poor people die every day from easily treatable ailments that require inexpensive medication and basic sanitation. You could personally bankroll a pastor in a third world country or finance the drilling of a water well for the price of a purebred puppy. That's the purchase price, not the total, long term cost. Why not adopt instead, or opt-out of pet ownership entirely?

I've traveled to dozens of remote mission bases in foreign countries with flimsy walls and scant furnishings.

Every one of them would benefit greatly from a trip to a hardware store with a generous person like yourself. Even secondhand furniture would be a big help. The humble leaders who operate in these far-flung outposts rarely have enough money, but they love the Lord and lay down their lives for the poor.

Impoverished missionaries often boil a kettle for bathing water. You're missing out if you haven't taken a bucket bath on a cold morning in an uninsulated house. Hot showers aren't possible without wealthy benefactors. Most of the missionaries I've met could find higher paying jobs elsewhere, but they serve out of love.

They earnestly pray for their monthly provisions, but that's not as romantic as it sounds. While rich in faith, their good works are severely limited by a shortage of generosity back home. Instead of giving until it hurts, most of us drop a small donation in the offering plate. Then, administration costs eat up most of the money.

Only a small fraction of our donations make it to the mission field on average. (6, 7) When all is said and done, we silently recite this verse to ourselves. "God causes all things to work together for good to those who love God, to those who are called according to His purpose." -Romans 8:28 NASB

I've seen an alarming number of Christians twist that verse into secular fatalism, which is the opposite of Christianity. Complacency isn't God's will or purpose, we all have free will. If someone doesn't feel led to labor in the harvest, they call it God's will. They might feel a bit guilty at times, but not enough for a major lifestyle change.

God will make a way when there seems to be no way. That's true, but why pray for someone else to provide what we can easily do ourselves? (James 2:1-13) In a healthy marriage, both sides give 100%, and the same is true with a good business partnership. God could do everything supernaturally, but then we wouldn't learn or grow.

Don't wait until you feel led. If you haven't done anything lately, go now, do something, anything. God will direct the steps of the righteous as you learn to recognize the sound of His voice. I pray that every Christian would read a few old missionary books and catch the fire and inspiration from previous generations.

Missionaries have a running joke about the joys of "blessed poverty" but a lack of funding doesn't help them any more than it would help your business or family. Have you ever prayed to experience intense poverty because it would strengthen your faith? I don't think so. I've met hundreds of independent missionaries, and I can't recall one who didn't dream about having better facilities with cupboards full of food, extra Bibles to share, and a surplus of medical supplies.

We love to say everything happens for a reason, but the main reason is an overall lack of generosity. If we're being honest, it feels good to spend money on what's right in front of us. As the darkness grows deeper, we need all hands on deck to fight the war against depression and despair.

"Why are you in despair, O my soul? And why are you disturbed within me? Hope in God, for I shall again praise Him, The help of my countenance and my God." -Psalm 43:4 NASB

"Vets first began prescribing Prozac for dogs around 1990, and it's likely a more common practice today than it was even 10 years ago. In 2012 alone, an estimated 2.8 million dog owners gave their dogs calming or anxiety medicines." - American Pet Products Association

When I lived in Southern California, I couldn't help but marvel at the big, beautiful, 24/7 veterinary offices near my home in Los Angeles. I'll never forget the first time I walked into a vet clinic with my dogs, it was in Santa Monica, not far from Beverly Hills. Everything was spotless, the facility was beautiful, the workers were friendly, and I didn't have to wait very long.

I arrived around ten or eleven at night, but the staff didn't look sleepy or sluggish. They had a large, building on a prime piece of real estate. The entire experience was phenomenal, I walked away after midnight smiling and carrying free samples of overpriced dog food. I've always been a bit of a night owl, and it seems like, no matter where I go, I don't have trouble finding a late night vet.

Going to the vet is one thing, going to a 24/7 vet clinic is another, but where do you draw the line with optional (non-emergency) medical expenses? For example, do you find a way to justify spending $70 a month for puppy Prozac? I'm not a fan of humans taking elective mood medication, let alone Pugs on drugs. We've gone overboard with drugs and I think it's time to dial it back a bit.

It's estimated that millions of Americans regularly purchase prescription pills and injections for their dogs. A lifetime supply of doggy downers might keep your Jack Russell Terrier from destroying the sofa, but a bottle of chill pills does nothing to address the underlying issue. Plus, it may be difficult to determine if you will end up spending more on pills or new furniture and slippers.

If a high energy dog is locked inside the house too much, there's no need to search high and low for the underlying issue. The answer is obvious, your dog needs more stimulation and physical activity. Dogs crave exercise, but lazy sloths and workaholics alike refuse to make time for long walks in the park or fun games in the yard with tennis balls and Frisbee discs.

Believe it or not, your sheepdog would rather be herding a flock of sheep right now. God created her to enjoy vigorous activities. Most dogs want to work, they don't want to be stuck inside alone all day, whacked out on mind-altering psychotropic drugs. If you're seriously considering the pros and cons of anti-depressants for your pets, then it's not about the dog. It's all about you and your dogged search for a quick fix that won't interrupt your schedule.

What is the best way to care for pets without compromising our convictions? Dogs are fun-loving, highly social animals, that's why we enjoy their company. Dogs want to play in the grass and run with the pack. Spend more time outside. A little more sunshine will help your health too. Think about this objectively, if you enjoyed walking 20 miles per day, how would you feel about being stuck inside an apartment 23.5 hours each day?

Except for certain small breeds, most dogs can cover ten miles in an hour, others can travel fifty miles in a day. How does that compare with being stuck in an apartment or a kennel? When a dog spends the majority of its life in a crate, that's equal to solitary confinement in prison, which is one of the worst punishment allowed in the American prison system.

According to the law, such treatment can border on psychological torture, and as such, it can only be used sparingly. (13) Even the worst criminals aren't supposed to be locked up alone forever because that is cruel and unusual punishment. In the wild, dogs fight for survival, but at least they're not alone. In nature, dogs aren't diabetic, neurotic, or strung out on drugs.

I think most dogs would rather fend for themselves in the wild, with their pack, if the only alternative was a long, lonely life in a cage. Dogs enjoy having a big yard, but if that isn't possible, it's better to pick a small breed or wait until your situation improves.

If you only have one dog, you might want to consider adopting another so they can play together. From what I've seen, the addition of one extra pup usually makes life better, not worse. If your current dog is old and the other is young, it can be difficult. Usually, they absorb each other's energy and play together with an intensity that humans cannot match. I know the thought of having a second dog may seem overwhelming, but if you can comfortably afford one, then you can probably handle two or three.

It's not a heavy burden unless you insist upon spending unlimited amounts of money on things like boarding and medical treatments. It's OK to set firm limits, that's the kind of self-control that leads to more freedom. I will not drop my family into a risky financial situation by giving my pets an unlimited, unconditional blank check for life.

If that's a deal-breaker for you, then it's best to stick with volunteering at a local animal shelter or visiting a friend who has dogs until you have more money in the bank. Here's another idea; apply for a part-time job in the pet industry, and try to find one that offers paid training. Do something practical to gain experience and extra income. Dog groomers earn a lot of money because it's a dirty job. Consider starting a dog walking business or train to be a dog trainer. Those are fun opportunities for anyone who understands the value of workplace evangelism and discipleship. It'll also help you understand the true cost of dog ownership.

We want to have it both ways, regardless of the contradictions or hypocrisy. If this sounds unreasonable, I would like to recommend you take a little time to reconsider your attitude towards drugs. Do you think it's OK to numb your pain all the time, or is there a positive purpose in the pain we experience? Drugs can numb a lot more than our muscles, and even the most beneficial medicine can be abused.

Isn't it best to remain as mentally sharp as possible, even if that means more pain at times? I've spoken to recovering drug addicts who said the best thing that ever happened (in regards to physical and emotional healing) was their choice to break free from pain and mood medication. There's a beautiful song by *Jimmy Eat world* that says; "If only you could see the stranger next to me, you promise you promise that you're done, but I can't tell you from the drugs."

I'm grateful for the times I've needed medication, but at a certain point, the cure can be worse than the disease. I wasted several years trying to numb my pain in various ways, but Jesus Christ is the only reason I'm sober, healthy, and content today. He set me free from depression and addiction. After a long season in the wilderness, I can say with confidence that His peace, joy, and love transcends all human understanding.

Are you willing to try the difficult solutions before taking the easy way out? Long-suffering and patience are required in most aspects of life. Consider the obesity epidemic in the Western world, those statistics should not define your story. The hardest choice is a drastic lifestyle change in terms of diet and exercise. If you have the mind of Christ, you can do all things.

Most of us know that eating fresh fruits, nuts, vegetables, and beans are by far the healthiest choice, but it's rare to see someone embrace a plant based diet. I've been to plenty of Christian pot luck dinners with zero veggies and dozens of dessert dishes. Fad diets, vitamin pills, and meal replacement bars are not good enough. I'm far from perfect, but I was able to lose over 30 pounds and keep it off with a healthier diet and an occasional Daniel fast. (Daniel ch1, Ch10)

We will cover that more in chapter 20, but my success was mainly due to abstaining from meats, sweets, salty snacks, and processed food. I did away with soft drinks, beer, refined sugar, and artificial sweeteners. I always feel better after a few days of eating raw vegetables, fruits, nuts, legumes, (beans) and sprouted grain bread. It's not expensive when you buy in bulk. Especially when you're used to paying fast food convenience prices. I heard a great quote once, "if you think education is expensive, try ignorance."

The same is true with diet and exercise. It won't solve all your problems, but if you think eating healthy and going to the gym is expensive, just ask a doctor how much it costs to die slowly from a preventable disease.

The true cost of sloth and gluttony stretches far beyond the mountain of money that's wasted on prescription pills, doctor's visits, and surgery. Great fortunes, (both in this age and the one to come) are routinely surrendered by decades of low energy, chronic pain, unnecessary suffering, and a drastically shortened life. Everyone should go to the gym more often and eat a ton of fresh, raw veggies.

If you're willing to make a few sacrifices, almost anyone can afford to buy bulk items like fresh fruit, vegetables, dry beans and brown rice. Instead of being smart with our money, an extreme devotion to the god of convenience is pursued with gusto. Food becomes a drug, especially sugar.

In the Bible, we can see the importance of fasting and prayer, but cultural Christians view fasting as unreasonable and legalistic. I know tough guys aren't scared of dying before their time (Ecclesiastes 7:17) but checking out early is foolish, cowardly, and that isn't the worst part.

Most preventable diseases destroy the immune system, leading to death by a thousand cuts. Every little sickness requires a longer recovery and possible complications. That high level of pain will easily break down the strongest man alive. Why not fall to your knees now, instead of being crushed completely when you least expect it? "And he who falls on this stone will be broken to pieces; but on whomever it falls, it will scatter him like dust." - Matthew 21:44 NASB

We want a pill to solve our problems, and that's such a cliché, but the teenage version of you would've been insulted if anyone suggested permanently sedating yourself or a house pet. I'm not talking about baby aspirin, catnip or herbal remedies. If you need a doctor's note or a drug dealer, then you're dealing with pharmakeia.

Pharmakeía

(from pharmakeuō, "administer drugs") – properly, drug-related sorcery, like the practice of magical-arts, etc. -A. T. Robertson

"Wake up from your drunken stupor, as is right, and do not go on sinning. For some have no knowledge of God. I say this to your shame." -1 Corinthians 15:34 ESV

That definition of pharmakeia (specifically, the use of medicine, drugs, or spells) does not mean that medicine is evil. Not at all. The Greek Biblical word is presented here to let you know about a double-edged sword that can be used for evil and also good. It's a caution and a warning. It's like a kitchen knife, you could use it to make fajitas, or you could hurt someone. What you do with inanimate objects is entirely up to you. They aren't good or evil, and they make a lousy scapegoat.

When it comes to drugs, you alone (not your physician) are responsible for what goes inside your body. No one puts a gun to your head whether we're talking about allergy medicine or the latest, greatest prescription on the market. No one is stopping you from reading a little research or seeking a second opinion. A doctor's note cannot absolve you from stewardship, responsibility, or consequences.

We can't blame anyone else for our own decisions. That's true whether or not your favorite drug is legal. What you're doing isn't automatically beneficial just because it's legal in your area. It's the principle of sowing and reaping, which has more to do with heart motives. That's the why behind what you're doing. "I the LORD search the heart and examine the mind, to reward each person according to their conduct, according to what their deeds deserve." -Jeremiah 17:10 NIV

If you follow the money, it isn't hard to discern the treasure of your heart. Don't feel bad if you've been lulled to sleep (or a drug-induced stupor) by pharmakeia. I'll explain why the deck is stacked against the consumer, but don't give up hope. Freedom is within reach for anyone who repents and turns from their sinful ways. Today is the best day to gird up your loins and stop making excuses.

The mainstream media profits handsomely from pharmaceutical ads. The media executives who profit the most couldn't care less about you or your health. Drug ads are repeated so often, it's overwhelming to the point that it has quickly changed our culture's attitude towards self-control and personal responsibility. The talking heads on TV tell us what to believe, but they directly profit from that ad revenue. That's a clear conflict of interest.

Instead of questions their legitimacy or motives, we ask our doctor about the latest, greatest bottle of pills. Instead of telling the truth, the big media players keep their sponsors happy by giving them a free pass whenever possible. To make matters worse, celebrity news personalities do their best to smear and discredit independent journalists who have little from gain by telling the truth.

Magazine publishers print an endless supply of uncritical content that places the pharmaceutical industry on a pedestal. When a terrible drug like Vioxx is pulled from the market, they jump on the bandwagon, but it's common knowledge that major media producers are reluctant to bite the hand that feeds.

"I ate breakfast last week with the president of a network news division and he told me that during non-election years, 70% of the advertising revenues for his news division come from pharmaceutical ads. And if you go on TV any night and watch the network news, you'll see they become just a vehicle for selling pharmaceuticals. He also told me that he would fire a host who brought onto his station a guest who lost him a pharmaceutical account." -Robert F. Kennedy Jr.

A major portion of the media's budget is funded by

pharmaceutical companies that invest far more into marketing than research. (11) They spend tens of billions to each year to influence doctors and around six billion on advertisements annually. Pills are pushed on TV and radio commercials all day, every day in America, but those same ads are strictly forbidden in almost every other nation. It's unethical to push drugs on the unsuspecting viewers, that's why it's illegal. The power of suggestion, combined with the assumed integrity of the mainstream media negatively influences the decisions of overly trusting (and weak-willed) people. (2 Timothy 3:6)

When the average person becomes sick in most nations, they call or visit a medical professional for recommendations. If someone in America or New Zealand isn't feeling well, they're likely to confront their doctor with forceful opinions that could interfere with a physician's objectivity and professionalism. If that doesn't work, they might shop around for a doctor who says what they want to hear. Immature believers do the same thing when we don't like what our pastor is teaching.

Drug companies are the undisputed world champions of selling. Their flashy branding and marketing campaigns are painstakingly crafted by the top firms. They do everything within their power to normalize a life that's anything but normal. Big Pharma is the most profitable segment of the healthcare business, which is the most profitable industry in the world.

At the same time, unpaid medical bills are the leading cause of bankruptcy in America. (12) How does that fit with a Hippocratic oath that swears to do no harm? Medical expenses account for 50-60% of all bankruptcies each year. Among those who file for bankruptcy, most have health insurance.   After all of that, I hope you can see why we should be careful about how we spend money. I want to have the faith of a child that Jesus described in Matthew 18:3. I want to be found faithful in every way when it's time to stand before God on judgment day. "choose this day whom you will serve... But as for me and my house, we will serve the LORD." -Joshua 24:15 ESV

Every time we make a decision and choose to do something, it limits our other options. You can't help everyone and you can't donate to every worthy cause. You can't trust that everyone or anyone has your best interests in mind, so it's important to be shrewd and wise about what goes into your body.

Every dollar that's spent today is gone, it can't be used again tomorrow. Every fleeting moment that's wasted over here, can never be reused over there. A choice to do something is also a choice to abstain from everything else at that moment.

Chapter 15

Cosmetic surgery for camels

"Every year, consumers in rich countries waste almost as much food (222 million tonnes) as the entire net food production of sub-Saharan Africa (230 million tonnes)." - FAO.org

"You shall not bring the fee of a prostitute or the wages of a dog into the house of the LORD your God in payment for any vow, for both of these are an abomination to the LORD your God." -Deuteronomy 23:18 ESV

Truth is stranger than fiction folks, and if you think the zoolatry train has reached its final destination, you're in for a surprise. Hold on tight and enjoy the ride, but before we move on to the next half of our study on modern idols, I would like to turn our attention to a few of the craziest trends that I found while researching for this book.

Cosmetic surgery is now common among top show animals. An overly ambitious pet owner can hire a plastic surgeon for a facelift or a tummy tuck to help win a big contest. It all goes back to the idols of greed, pride, and vain ambition. The world's top animal competitions have cash prizes in the millions. The battle is so fierce that illegal Botox injections have become a regular problem at major events. (13)

Steroid doping scandals are nothing new in the world of Greyhound racing, and dog tracks have been shut down due to allegations of extreme abuse and live-baiting, which is a method of torturing live 'bait' animals to improve a racing dog's predatorial instincts. (15) Even if you don't care about races or beauty pageants, there's a lot of evil happening behind closed doors.

Next, hundreds of thousands of dog owners have spent a fortune for silicone testicle implants, which are called neuticles. Purchasing surgical implants after neutering your male dog is advertised as a way to help dogs (read: owner) feel better about the removal of his testicles. Other popular procedures for dogs include nose jobs, eye lifts, liposuction and more.

Cosmetic surgery for animals began with the idiotic practice of cropping ears and docking tails. Just in case science isn't your strong suit, a dog's tail is an extension of its spine. The docking procedure sounds like it would the most painful thing imaginable. It's a barbaric practice that's illegal in most of Europe, and can permanently alter a dog's nervous system, balance, and gait. Since it's a breed standard, it's embraced without a second thought for the animal's overall well being.

Did God make a mistake when He created your Cocker Spaniel? The advocates for tail docking act like they don't have a choice. So they chop off the tail of certain breeds, under the assumption that a dog couldn't possibly make it through life without losing their tail in a freak accident. It's more than controversial, The American Veterinary Medical Association (AVMA), and other organizations oppose tail docking with few exceptions.

"A 2010 survey of almost 140,000 dogs in Great Britain (where dog tail docking is illegal), revealed that the risk that a dog would injure its tail in its lifetime was only 0.23 percent. That means 500 dogs would need to be docked to prevent one injury. And, far more would be required to prevent an injury serious enough to require amputation." - Trainthatpooch.com

After suffering through the first half of this book, I can only imagine how bizarre all of this must seem to someone who wasn't raised on a steady diet of Western news and entertainment. From the perspective of any ordinary, working-class person from the 18th or 19th century, we would probably look like the crazy rich people from the *Hunger Games*.

If you haven't seen the movies just search online for pictures of the characters from Capitol City or watch a few clips on YouTube. They were the villains in the films and book series. They had ridiculously ornate hairstyles and outrageously impractical clothing. They were beyond ostentatious, but within their self-affirming echo chambers, they saw themselves as normal.

The residents of Capitol City were shallow, petty, vain, and effeminate. They were the kind of people who lit their cigars with hundred dollar bills and enjoyed watching half-starved peasants fight to the death on TV for sport. I'd imagine that's what it was like back in the days of the Colosseum in Rome. King Solomon was right when he said: "there's nothing new under the sun". -Ecclesiastes 1:9

The Romans had a philosophy called *Bread and Circuses*, and it's happening again today. Roman leaders believed that society (I'm using the term loosely) could avoid civil unrest as long as commoners had plenty of food and entertainment. It was a distraction to keep the masses docile. Looking at the world today, it doesn't seem to matter if politicians are corrupt and inept, our focus seems to be painfully self-centered and nearsighted.

We might talk a good game about changing the world, but as long as the A/C blows cold air, the Internet works, and there's food in the fridge, most of us won't fight for change. We're engrossed with hobbies and habits that have become addictions and idols. *The Hunger Games* may be a dystopian fiction, but it's a lot closer to home than we'd like to admit.

Injustice in the real world can be as bleak as the movies, but please, visit Yemen or Somalia if you think I'm exaggerating. Have you ever watched a hot dog eating contest on TV? Can you eat seventy hot dogs in ten minutes or less? If so, you could win a cash prize. Or, instead of that, you could invite a few friends over and cook enough food to feed seventy or eighty underprivileged kids.

Many youth groups in America play the chubby bunny game, and I wish they would stop. Some youth pastors will say I'm making a big deal over nothing. Even so, I stand by my conviction that it's vulgar, asinine, and teaches kids to be wasteful.

If you aren't familiar with the game, it involves stuffing your face with as many marshmallows as possible, and trying to talk with your mouth full. Whoever crams the most while being able to say "chubby bunny" wins. After that, you spit them out and start over again.

Yes, I understand marshmallows are cheap, that's beside the point. Pastors are fond of saying "our lowest standard will be their highest standard." So then we agree, it's the small foxes that spoil the vine. Youth group is supposed to be fun at times. I've led one long enough to understand the need for balance and camaraderie. So let the good times roll so long as we keep Christ at the center.

If you lead games of chubby bunny, but you've never sponsored a youth group field trip to serve local soup kitchens, shelters, etc., then there's a hole in your Gospel. Let's lead by example and teach kids to be like Jesus. There are millions of people in poor places like Haiti who would shed tears of joy if they could eat the food that falls to the floor in a pie-eating contest.

Do you think they have mud cake eating contests in Haiti? You know about mud cakes, right? They're made with dirt, water, sugar, and oil. That's what the poorest of the poor eat in Haiti when they can't find work or scrounge up enough money to buy real food. It's hard to comprehend the extremes of poverty that lead to such a tragedy. A little child who was created in the image of God is eating a mud cake right now, while we live in luxury. Wouldn't it be nice to help more people by consuming less and creating more?

Chapter 16

PART 2

Jobs and Other idols

"Most people know you can make a god out of money. Most know you can make a god out of sex. However, anything in life can serve as an idol, a god-alternative, a counterfeit god…We think that idols are bad things, but that is almost never the case. The greater the good, the more likely we are to expect that it can satisfy our deepest needs and hopes." - Tim Keller

"Their land is filled with silver and gold, and there is no end to their treasures; their land is filled with horses, and there is no end to their chariots. Their land is filled with idols; they bow down to the work of their hands, to what their own fingers have made." -Isaiah 2:7,8 ESV

The first part of this book is a case study on idolatry as it relates to domestic animals. Let's give your dog a break and shift our focus to other common idols. We've gone deep, now let's go wide. From here on, we won't need to spend as much time on any specific idol. By this point, the hope is that you're able to apply these general lessons to your situation, even if we don't mention your idol by name.

At the end of the day, idols are more similar than different. (1 Corinthians 10:13) The particulars of your pitfall aren't nearly as important as the fact that God can deal with it swiftly and effortlessly. The redemption found in Christ alone is more powerful than any force on Earth. It should be clear by now that idolatry is the manifestation of most life-controlling sins. God spoke once and for all against idolatry on Mount Sinai. The original ten commandments were inscribed by the very hand of God. (Exodus 32:19)

Our creator left no room for ambiguity, His words were written in stone. No other gods, no graven images, no coveting, no exceptions. (Exodus ch 20) Why so many rules? God has the bird's eye view and wisdom that we lack. It's not about rules, it's about the freedom and joy that comes from holiness.

Jesus was kind and loving, but He has never been a pushover. Therefore, friendship with God should be pursued earnestly, not presumed upon arrogantly. If you're still reading this book by now, then I think that demonstrates a commitment to overcoming idolatry, no matter the cost. I pray that God will empower you to help set others free as you recover from your past mistakes.

You don't have to be an expert to share the Good News. As one hand washes the other, so we should start right where we are, and help hold each other accountable with love and all humility. My prayer is that cultural (nominal) Christians will read this book and commit their lives to authentic Christianity.

This book was written for anyone who craves freedom, peace, and joy. Christians believe in Jesus as best as they have been taught, but most of us are not living for God, not in any meaningful way. We each do what we think is best by our standards of right and wrong. I constantly meet believers who are willfully stuck in a prison of sin.

Take some time to reconsider the fruit of your labors. It's not just about doing what's right, it's also important to recognize the times and seasons. Ask God to help you hear His voice and to help you judge clearly between what's good, better, and best. Don't waste your time with something that's just OK when you could be doing something much more important and meaningful with your free time.

How can you tell when something (or someone) has become an idol? I should point out that there are gray areas, so please give yourself a big dose of grace. What may be appropriate for you in your circumstances, might not be a good idea for me. I'm not talking about explicit sin, but rather permissible choices that may not be beneficial.

As we mature, God gives greater revelation to those who pursue Him. Your conscience may have allowed you to get away with something questionable five years ago, but as your mature it will not sit well with you anymore. Luckily, we have the gift of the Holy Spirit to convict and edify. I do know one thing; if loosing that certain something would crush you, then it's probably an idol. If you spend a lot of time and money on something nonessential that keeps you away from ministry and other important relationships, then it's probably an idol.

That doesn't make your favorite pastime inherently evil, but it's best to lay it down for a while until you've strengthened your relationship with the Lord and picked up a few good habits. Remember, one extreme is just as bad as the other. So be careful when you're making adjustments in life. I've seen people trade one bad habit for 'the lesser of two evils' and pretend like that's God's will. Don't be the guy who trades heavy drinking for heavy smoking, or the woman who trades trashy TV shows for trashy romantic novels.

The devil wins whenever you're locked into an unhealthy lifestyle, and there's a big ditch on either side of the narrow path. From what I've seen, workplace idolatry is socially acceptable. However, we don't want to overcorrect or over-spiritualize to the point that we frown upon an honest day's work just because someone close to us has taken it too far. "Let the thief no longer steal, but rather let him labor, doing honest work with his own hands, so that he may have something to share with anyone in need." -Ephesians 4:28 ESV

It's wrong to demonize your day job as much as it is wrong to idolize your career (or to covet someone else's achievements). I could fill a large book with stories about wasted lives and marriages sacrificed on the altar of corporate greed, but there's no need. If you are neck deep into career idolatry, I'm probably not the first person to point out the fact that you've become a workaholic.

Most of us only need to make a few small adjustments to our schedule. A few hours here, a few hours there can be a good start. Some of us need to leave work a little earlier each day, but others need to work much harder and smarter, that all depends on your own natural tendencies. In some cases, you might have to step down altogether and take a low stress position somewhere else, even if that means downsizing your house and cars.

Sabbaticals are not just for clergy, you might benefit from taking off next summer or slowing down your pace with an extended Christmas break. It's funny how people turn their winter break into a crazy, stressful flurry of activities. That's not God's will for your life. What if you rested more during your vacation? Now that's a revolutionary idea. Instead of buying a bunch of stuff and running around doing all the things, you could spend time relaxing and restoring your soul. (Psalm 23)

No matter how you pay the bills, Jesus has called you to be a "fisher of men" (Matthew 4:19). Ironically, I think most men would rather stick with catching fish and leave the work of evangelism to someone else. Are you addicted to the salt life? Americans spend seventy billion dollars each year on recreational saltwater fishing according to NOAA.gov.

Those figures don't include freshwater or commercial fishing, competitions, fishing apparel, video games, or TV revenue. Fishing is fun and relaxing, but when it becomes an idol, it hurts everyone within your circle of influence. Your family (and church family) wants to spend time with you, and that requires a big dose of selflessness. I feel close to God when I'm surrounded by nature, but even so, a life devoted to leisure is a life wasted.

Jesus spoke about the pearl of great price, which is a perfect analogy of your situation. (Matthew 13:46) If you had to trade everything you owned to buy one, priceless, rare jewel, would you do it? Of course you would. Jesus Christ is the pearl of great price. Or, if you prefer, the pearl is a metaphor for your relationship with Jesus. That's a gift you can help someone attain through discipleship. If Heaven is real, why wouldn't we want to be fishers of men? Idols don't share, they demand loyalty, but Jesus said no one can serve two masters. (Matthew 6:24)

"human beings have a deep need to bond and form connections. It's how we get our satisfaction. If we can't connect with each other, we will connect with anything we can find — the whirr of a roulette wheel or the prick of a syringe... we should stop talking about 'addiction' altogether, and instead call it 'bonding.' A heroin addict has bonded with heroin because she couldn't bond as fully with anything else. So the opposite of addiction is not sobriety. It is human connection." -Johann Hari

If I hired a research team to follow you around 24/7, what would they say? I'm talking about fair, impartial observers with access to every phone call, text message, app, websites visited, and bank statement. What would investigative reporters say after a few weeks on your trail? If you feel convicted about your Internet search history or cash purchases, maybe it's time to make a few changes.

When I was having a hard time overcoming idolatry, I canceled my Internet service at home for six months. During that time, if something was urgent, I went to my office or a coffee shop to use their wifi. Big steps like this can be a real lifesaver whether you're hooked on Netflix, sports, gambling, pornography or video games. You might need to sell your smartphone or set it to black and white mode (grayscale) to make it less appealing. (16)

Remove unnecessary apps, uninstall your favorite games, and embrace a bit of old fashioned disciple. When you "catch the small foxes" it will help you refrain from checking Facebook a million times each day. I have friends who have traveled to remote monasteries and signed up to work on a farm all summer. Do whatever it takes, even if it's a weekend camping trip to reset your natural sleep cycle.

How can anyone "seek and save the lost" if they're floundering in a sea of sin? Landing that dream job won't solve your problems. Without a firm foundation in Christ, all that extra money and influence will only magnify your problems. If you don't believe me just ask anyone who's won the lottery. (17) Americans spend over $80 billion on lottery tickets each year and based on everything I've read, the lotto is essentially a tax on the poor.

When you want to see the truth, the dots are easy to connect. Gluttony idolizes food, sloth idolizes relaxation, and lust makes an idol of sex. Hollywood teaches us to idolize youth and beauty. When parents and grandparents live vicariously through their kids or grandkids, that's idolatry too.

The worship of children is difficult to overcome because it's an overreaction to the mistakes of workaholics. It's common among those who didn't receive much attention from their parents. The Old Testament story of Eli shows us what can happen when parents idolize their kids. (1 Samuel ch 2)

Another possibility is that Eli was so busy with his official duties that he didn't make time for his kids, and that may have contributed to their decline. By the time the boys were all grown up, his sons couldn't have cared less about their father's opinions or authority. Whatever the reasons, it led to the humiliation and destruction of Eli's family.

Workaholics ignore the needs of their children (and the church) for the sake of money or prestige. They say they're working for their family, but that's deception. What your spouse and kids really want is more time together as a family. Your church needs mentors and big brothers who are successful in business. If your family doesn't want to be around you at this point, then you've got your work cut out for you. That's an even more compelling reason to change your life for the better.

Little kids don't care about vacation homes, fancy cars or big houses in gated neighborhoods. Teenagers start to care about materialism with the help of parents, peers and the media they consume. You can't win every battle, but you can overcome the temptations that will set you up for failure. Do you abide in Christ, or are you comforted by the size of your bank account?

On another note, contemporary Christians are fond of saying "my children are my mission field" which sounds super-spiritual, but it's usually an excuse for inactivity in regards to teaching, preaching, outreach, and evangelism, etc. I don't think God leads anyone to 'set aside the ministry' until their kids are fully grown. God will never give you a personal revelation that contradicts the Bible

"Train up a child in the way he should go, Even when he is old he will not depart from it." -Proverbs 22:6 NASB

"God bless me and my wife, My son and his wife, Us four and no more. Amen." -Unknown

Teach your kids to be productive and charitable, that's the takeaway from Proverbs 22:6. This particular Proverb directly contradicts any excuses that, by the way, only sounds reasonable to lukewarm Christians. Choosing to look after you and your family alone isn't mission work, it's the textbook definition of being self-centered.

Don't shelter your kids from reality, that's a disservice. Teach kids by escorting them to a local charity. Don't take a twenty-year hiatus from the harvest, go do something useful today. The type of ministry might shift for the sake of your tender little ones, but it doesn't need to stop altogether.

My wife and I volunteered to help with Sunday school when our first child turned two. It was a precious experience, and it's hard to describe how much I learned by babysitting ten or fifteen toddlers every Sunday morning. This was a tender season, and it was absolutely beautiful.

You don't have to drop your kids into a war zone just to make them tough, but you should introduce them to ministries that help those who are facing extreme poverty. They can handle the truth because God created them for such a time as this.

I think the reason so many pastor's kids (and others) walk away from church entirely is because they see too much church business, conflict, and hypocrisy, but a lack of deliverance, miracles, or Good News preached to the poor.

If you took your kids to an inner city mission base once in a while, I think most would benefit from such a radically different perspective compared to boring, safe, suburban Christianity. If you want your kids to love Jesus when they are older, then get your hands dirty and lead by example. Teenagers have zero tolerance for hypocrisy, so reconsider your priorities if that's what it takes to be more authentic.

We can become very busy with menial tasks that have nothing to do with the Great Commission. Busyness for the sake of busyness leaves us little time for what matters the most, our love for the Lord and each other. Religion itself and religious duties can become an idol. How can anyone attend church for decades without being a real Christian? I don't know, but unfortunately, it happens all the time.

In our modern era, it's socially expedient to call yourself a Christian (in the Western world). If we aren't careful, church gatherings can be reduced to networking opportunities or just another social event. Church attendance comes with perks, and that's OK, but what happens when God's sacred temple becomes a den of robbers? We will discuss that in chapter 22.

I can't blame anyone for making the most of their situation, but if you constantly take but never give until it hurts, it's proof that you don't know Jesus, and that's true even if you know all about Jesus. If you're going through the motions of religious duties, then you probably haven't experienced the power of His love. It's time to stop playing church. Take the New Testament as your personal blueprint for success, because the Word of God has never been more relevant.

Chapter 17

Golden calves and the silver screen

"According to a 2013 Policy Statement by the American Academy of Pediatrics, 8- to 10 year-olds spend 8 hours a day with various digital media while teenagers spend 11 hours in front of screens... Dr. Peter Whybrow, director of neuroscience at UCLA, calls screens "electronic cocaine" and Chinese researchers call them "digital heroin." In fact, Dr. Andrew Doan, the head of addiction research for the Pentagon and the US Navy — who has been researching video game addiction — calls video games and screen technologies "digital pharmakeia" (Greek for drug)... In addition, hundreds of clinical studies show that screens increase depression, anxiety and aggression and can even lead to psychotic-like features where the video gamer loses touch with reality." -Dr. Nicholas Kardaras

"If you find honey, eat just enough-- too much of it, and you will vomit." -Proverbs 25:16 NIV

If I had to guess, I'd say the most socially acceptable idol today is television. We know that small foxes spoil the vine, but TV addiction is the pink elephant in the room that no one wants to acknowledge. By the way, whenever I say TV it's meant to include all screens, no matter the size. You might favor a smartphone, tablet, desktop computer or a giant projector with surround sound, but idolatry is possible with any screen.

Meanwhile, pastors and ministry leaders struggle to find a few brave souls who can muster the stamina that's required for brief, weekly prayer meetings. How hard can it be? Millions of Christians are uncontrollably addicted to their precious little TV screen. It's a virtual prison full of fantasy and entirely devoid of reality.

We soak up 'good preaching' as if it were a spectator sport, and many of us have stopped going to church because we're offended and it's easier to watch sermons online at home in your pajamas. Instead of joining in the plentiful harvest, the silent majority clings to the safety and comfort of their living room while occasionally venturing outside for fellowship when it suits our mood.

TV's are cheap and plentiful. You can watch thousands of streaming channels and browse through a never ending list of nifty websites and apps. YouTube hosts over five billion videos at last count. After work, you can just sit back, relax and forget about your problems for a while.

Your TV screen provides a constant supply of artificial, one-way relationships that allow you to constantly take without giving anything in return. That's what we want out of idols, unconditional love with no effort required on our part and no strings attached. As we learned in the first part of this book, that's why we struggle with interpersonal relationships, humans are full of opinions and feelings who need respect, honor, and loyalty. Real relationships require a bit of risk and sacrifice, unlike the TV.

If zoning out in front of the TV like a zombie isn't your cup of tea, you can play video games that allow you to shoot zombies. If you aren't fond of simulating mass murder, you can rescue the princess by solving puzzles or collecting coins. Video games are fun and educational in small doses.

At least games force you to think quickly and make decisions. Instead of passively watching fantasy or adventure movies, video games give you control over those fictional characters. You get to direct the action, but at the end of the day, it's an imaginary game.

We watch TV to escape the drudgery and boredom of our daily life. Deep down inside, we want to be war heroes or pro athletes and rock stars. I grew up playing the first few Nintendo and Sega console's, but when I found the Lord I completely lost interest. I didn't have time for it anymore, and the desire was gone.

In Hollywood, professional screenwriters spend days drafting jokes and clever dialogue that's consumed by viewers in a short sitcom. Each line is skillfully delivered by beautiful actors who are surrounded by gorgeous scenery. If you prefer a gritty aesthetic, you can watch war documentaries or TV shows about pioneers climbing mountains. It's fun to daydream about being a popular person who always says the right thing and hangs out at cool places, but an endless stream of fantasy leads viewers to lose touch with reality.

The laugh track tells you when to laugh, which fools you into thinking you have a good sense of humor even if you're a grinch. The special effects lead you to believe that you have a healthy, vivid imagination but it's all passive consumption. In reality, constant stimulation stunts your mind as you gobble up content that others have created. Kids and adults alike cling to their smartphones in the same way that Linus from Peanuts used his comfort blanket and sucked on his thumb.

We love to watch shows featuring lippy lawyers who never loses an argument and silly sitcoms about fashionable, upper-middle-class families who resolve every conflict by the end of each episode. Believe it or not, a steady diet of entertainment is about a healthy as a steady diet of junk food. It alters your expectations and over time it leaves you less satisfied with your own life. The more you consume, the more you crave unrealistic, idealistic, escapism. That's also true with pornography addictions.

Too many sweets rot the teeth and too much screen time will crush your soul. The average Westerner can't handle silence so the TV (or radio) is always on in the background. I recently spoke with a friend who told me that he doesn't allow any silence in his life. By his own admission, he's afraid to be left alone with his thoughts. The TV helps him drown out painful memories with non-stop noise, news, and entertainment.

Bottle it up if you want, but sooner or later the dam will break and all those memories will flood into the forefront of your mind. It's better to fall on the rock now, before it happens unexpectedly, at the worst possible moment. The decision to reject silence isn't only a spiritual suicide. It cuts into your productivity and overall quality of life. Make a covenant with your eyes and keep yourself free from every kind of lust whether it's money, sex, power, the lust of the flesh, the lust of the eyes, or the pride of life. (1 John 2:16)

"I will not set before my eyes anything that is worthless." - Psalm 101:3 ESV

"When there's something in the Bible that churches don´t like, they call it 'legalism' How can you pull down strongholds of Satan if you don't even have the strength to turn off your TV?"
-Leonard Ravenhill

Over the past few years, I've visited churches that have employed off duty police officers and armed security guards to protect their congregation. Mass shootings at churches and synagogues have become commonplace and I think it's wise to have uniformed guards on site whenever possible. A visible security team can be an excellent deterrent for maniacs who prey on the weak, but that only works when the guards are paying attention.

I've noticed several watchmen neglecting their duty for the sake of their phones. I know because I hung around just to see if they were sending a quick text message. As the minutes ticked by it was clear to see that they were focused entirely on their phone. They stand around watching videos or who knows, maybe playing Candy Crush.

These men have sworn an oath to remain vigilant and protect the church, but if they were thrust into an active shooter emergency, they would be woefully unprepared. The ones I've seen were so oblivious that a bad guy could walk by with a bazooka or whack them on the head with a club before they bothered to look up from their precious little cellphone.

An amateur could easily get the drop on them and that's a disgrace. Watchmen have a sacred duty, and a big part of that is situational awareness. A lack of discipline can only be as bad as the congregation will tolerate. Everyone must do their part and anyone who's slacking on the job while being paid to protect the church should be removed immediately and replaced. Idols will destroy as much as we let them, it's time to reclaim the territory that we've forfeited. At church, most of us don't want to be seen as rude, but silence in the face of evil is as cowardly as it is dangerous.

"But if the watchman sees the sword coming and does not blow the trumpet, so that the people are not warned, and the sword comes and takes any one of them, that person is taken away in his iniquity, but his blood I will require at the watchman's hand." -Ezekiel 33:6 ESV

"33:1-9 The prophet is a watchman to the house of Israel. His business is to warn sinners of their misery and danger. He must warn the wicked to turn from their way, that they may live. If souls perish through his neglect of duty, he brings guilt upon himself." -Matthew Henry Commentary

I drive long distances for work, and every day I pass a dozen drivers or more with their heads tilted down toward their phones during rush hour traffic. If you drive a sales or delivery route or have a long commute, you've probably seen the same thing a thousand times. Using your phone while driving is dangerous and illegal in most places, but everyone sees themselves as an exception to the rules.

Why would anyone risk their life and the lives of others just to scroll through text messages and photos on Instagram? The only reasonable explanation is that it's an addiction equal to any narcotic. It feels good to see those notifications, and that tiny rush of dopamine spikes when people like your pictures and posts.

Well-educated, productive members of society are constantly taking brazen risks for a quick fix and that's flat out reckless. It's the kind of behavior you'd expect from a meth addict, not someone who has the mind of Christ. We need to start talking about screen time in terms of addiction and bonding. In this area, we have been too easy on ourselves.

God knows we aren't always compassionate about the sins of our enemies, but when it comes to our own sin, we expect a free pass and plenty of grace. In the past twenty-five years, I've driven in several different nations and almost all fifty states. From what I've seen, the attention span of drivers has only become worse over the years.

I am looking forward to self-driving cars which will be a real game changer. People are crazy. It's gotten to the point that now I'm forced to tap on my horn daily, not at aggressive drivers, (which was common in the past) but negligent, distracted drivers. It's happened several times in one day, where a person in front of me is looking down down (or I can see their bright screen) and the drives doesn't realize the traffic light has turned green. I frequently see drivers swerving out of their lane while looking at their phones.

If you look you can usually see the driver's head tilted down for extended lengths of time. At night, you can see the bright glowing screen up against the top of their steering wheel. They aren't even trying to hide it anymore.

Addiction is more than a deep craving for pleasure, entertainment, and escapism, it's a manifestation of loneliness. We have a deep longing to be part of a loving, close-knit community. God created us to be social but social media and other distractions have driven us to isolation. We desire action and adventure, but we settle for watching someone else's adventure on TV. God put that desire in your heart, so go for the real thing.

Throughout most of human history, very few people worked in the artificial conditions that are common today. We work in cubicles, warehouses, and factories, but we were created for so much more. Those jobs aren't bad, but it becomes a problem when we go straight home and plop onto the couch after work. It's not healthy to spend eight or nine hours in front of an office computer only to go home and watch five or six hours of TV.

Our vitality is crushed by the constant attrition of life, it can be subtle at times. We have to find healthier ways to rest and recharge. You might not be able to change jobs easily, and God may have you there for a reason, but you do have the power to turn off your TV and go for a walk. That's a great starting point. Your mental, emotional and spiritual health are all connected to your physical health. Don't let the weakest link ruin your potential in all other areas.

You will never know your potential as long as you are suffering from a lifestyle of bad choices. Whatever you do in life it's all connected. The food you eat, the way you sleep, what you allow yourself to watch and say, even your secret thought life, all of that is under your discretion. One idol is all it takes to keep you from having a healthy heart, mind, and body.

What good can a giant pile of money do if you're suffering from poor health and low energy? Instead of destroying your body to make a few bucks, try reducing your commitments and start eating healthy food. Stop watching TV and sign up for a gym membership. Show up five times a week and for at least one hour. Even when you don't have the energy or motivation, just force yourself to show up.

If you have a hard time with motivation, make drastic changes. Burn your boat, as they say. Cancel your cable, digital, or dish TV package and don't give yourself screen time unless you do so while riding a stationary bike or using the elliptical machines. I'm walking on a treadmill desk right now at my office. I also have a Desk Cycle that fits under my desk at home. It's a small cycling rig designed to fit under a desk. It's silent and allows me to peddle for hours while I'm stuck on long conference calls or chipping away at boring paperwork.

Small improvements like this have changed my life, it's not rocket science. My Desk Cycle improves my focus and it stimulates my metabolism. The best part is it alleviates my lower back pain which makes me more productive. That thing has paid for itself many times over. People say fitness is expensive, but walking is free and that's a great start.

The cost of an average TV bundle is higher than the price of most gym memberships. If you're broke, it's easy to find used gym equipment and free weights at garage sales or thrift shops for pennies on the dollar. My point here is simple; something is better than nothing. Do whatever it takes to improve your physical, mental, and emotional health now that you've abandoned your idols.

Find a pastoral counselor who can meet up once per week or a Christian life coach. Join a softball team or buy a pair of Rollerblades. As always, remember that sports can become a replacement idol if your heart isn't in the right place. There's no one size fits all formula or cookie-cutter solution. Seek the Lord on your hands and knees and whatever you do, watch less TV.

Chapter 18

Power in the airwaves

"And you were dead in the trespasses and sins in which you once walked, following the course of this world, following the prince of the power of the air, the spirit that is now at work in the sons of disobedience— among whom we all once lived in the passions of our flesh, carrying out the desires of the body and the mind, and were by nature children of wrath, like the rest of mankind" -Ephesian 2:1-3 ESV

"the phrase "the power of the air" is unique and difficult. We note that this phrase signifies not "a power over the air," but "a power dwelling in the region of the air." Now, the word "power" (see Note on Ephesians 1:21), both in the singular and the plural, is used in this Epistle, almost technically, of superhuman power. Here, therefore, the Evil One is described as "the prince," or ruler, of such superhuman power--considered here collectively as a single power, prevailing over the world, and working in the children of disobedience--in the same sense in which he is called the "prince of the devils," the individual spirits of wickedness (Matthew 9:34; Matthew 12:24)." -Ellicott's Commentary

In the book of Ephesians, there's a cryptic passage

that, in my opinion, sheds light on the entertainment industry and media in general. Our ancestors didn't have the missing puzzle pieces to comprehend the full meaning of this passage. The book of Daniel explains that mysteries will come to light in the latter days; "But you, Daniel, shut up the words and seal the book, until the time of the end. Many shall run to and fro, and knowledge shall increase." -Daniel 12:4 ESV

We know that there is nothing concealed that won't be disclosed, or hidden that will not be made known, (Luke 12:2) but we don't know exactly how that will occur. I think it will happen in a variety of creative ways. Knowledge will increase through the usual avenues of scientific advancement, along with dreams, visions, and personal revelations. When that happens, it forces us to work together as a team. "For we know in part and we prophesy in part..." -1 Corinthians 13:9 ESV

Now let's talk about "the ruler of the kingdom of the air". Other translations call this person the "prince of the power of the air" Why does this power dwell in the air? In context, we know it's the opposite of God's Kingdom. I searched through online Bible commentaries to look for plausible answers, but the only consensus seems to be that most scholars didn't exactly know what to do with this passage.

The classic commentaries were surprisingly skillful in their attempts to explain a phenomenon that would have been impossible to comprehend before the advent of modern technology. Perhaps this piece of the puzzle was hidden until now. What travels over the airwaves? TV, radio, satellites, etc.

This power is currently wielded by false prophets who pervert Christian values all day long. Mocking other religions and lifestyles is generally off-limits, but it's open season on Christians who refuse to abandon the Bible. Some have gone so far as to call mainstream media the false prophet from Revelation.

Six corporations that control about 90% of the media in America. (18) The days of objective (mainstream) journalism are gone. Radio stations, newspapers and popular magazines are almost entirely monopolized by a handful of major companies and the biggest websites are being purchased and consolidated as fast as possible.

Monopolies offer the illusion of choice, and viewers gobble it up. People mistakingly place their identity in lifeless brands, and some are willing to argue over their preference of music channels like MTV, BET or VH1, but at the end of the day, one billionaire owns all three companies. In my opinion, the primary goal isn't to profit or entertain, not anymore. Their goals are more sinister and it's hard to make sense of the trends until you accept the reality of an unseen spiritual battle where good is pitted against evil.

Media overlords tirelessly work to stir up dissension, twist the truth, and desensitize society. They say sensationalism sells, but that's only a partial truth. Media moguls intentionally alienate large blocks of viewers, and they aren't doing it to boost the ratings. They never have anything good to say about Christians, but Christians make up the largest portion of their viewer base. We rarely fight back and that stems from our collective acceptance of idolatry.

On the bright side, mainstream news outlets have declined in popularity recently. The overt attack against Christ and His followers is belligerent and demonic. Christians are the punching bag of the entertainment industry and it's intentional. If you don't believe the enemy has a strategy, that means his strategy is working on you.

Similarly, if you don't believe the mainstream media is systematically dumbing down their audience, then you may have been systematically dumbed down. It's called TV programming for a reason folks, and I know that's a hard pill to swallow, but rejecting the truth only makes you easier to fool. No other religion is brazenly mocked by Hollywood gatekeepers and elitists. If you don't bow your knee to Baal; which in modern terms means you refuse to "celebrate sin", it can destroy your career.

"The king answered Daniel and said, "Surely your God is a God of gods and a Lord of kings and a revealer of mysteries, since you have been able to reveal this mystery." - Daniel 2:47 NASB

The entertainment industry preaches a new kind of morality, and their version of the truth is frequently revised and rebooted. What will you do, are you the head or the tail? (Deuteronomy 28:13) Almost every local news channel that I've seen refuses to broadcast the positive accomplishments of local churches. I don't think I'm alone when I say I'd love to hear more good news.

Instead of reporting the good with the bad, the news entertainment overlords constantly lead with the obituaries. If it bleeds, it leads, so they broadcast the most gruesome headlines from around the world. If that isn't sick enough, they intentionally put a spotlight on the most obscure Christian cults. It's an important part of their God-hating smear campaign, and it won't stop until we demand change.

Reporters search high and low for mentally unstable pastors who make us look bad. TV producers latch onto hate-filled fanatics who are typically small-time, backwood nobodies who couldn't get fifteen minutes of fame without the media machine that props them up like a puppet.

If the mainstream media would simply ignore those lunatics, (like the rest of us) hardly anyone would know they exist. If there were a legitimate threat or a crime under investigation, then that's another story, but most of these shenanigans are the work of the accuser of the brethren. I've never seen a local news segment that was critical of Muslim, Hindu, or Buddhist clergy. That's against the rules. Even if you can find an exception, that doesn't disprove the rule.

Media moguls push the weirdo Christian narrative for one specific reason; to disparage Christians without the risk of legal repercussions. After all, they're just reporting the news and conducting honest interviews, right? It's hard to make a case for defamation or liable when they find a foolish pastor who's willing to spew venom in front of a camera.

The war that's raging over the airwaves isn't logical or reasonable. Can you think of any local business owner in your area who would willingly run a series of TV commercials that were offensive to a large portion of his viewers? No, that wouldn't be good for business. You don't have to be an advertising expert to understand that alienating and antagonizing Christians is foolish.

"Little children, you are from God and have overcome them, for he who is in you is greater than he who is in the world." - 1 John 4:4 ESV

On the bright side, high quality Christian media groups have emerged to fill the gap. Churches and other groups are constantly working to improve the quality of their content and blazing new trails. Online video broadcasting equipment is now more affordable than ever. That has opened the door for independent filmmakers and other artists who love the Lord.

Christians are beginning to wake up and realize they have healthier options. Consumers are slowly shifting their money over to wholesome streaming services like Pure Flix, Right Now Media, VidAngel, GodTV, MorningstarTV, various YouTube creators and my personal favorite, IHOPKC.org. We can expect to see this trend increase and it's very encouraging.

Mainstream media is a secular propaganda machine filled with highly editorialized headlines that tell you what to think. That's why I prefer to read news articles online and make an honest effort to avoid bias and sensationalism. Did you know that news anchors and reporters from previous generations devoted themselves to impartiality? When my parents were growing up, the most popular news stations demanded an impressive level of professionalism.

Forty of fifty years ago, the average American didn't know if his favorite news anchor leaned conservative or liberal. They saw themselves as public servants with a sacred trust and a solemn duty. They weren't perfect, but their commitment to neutrality puts most modern reporters to shame. Don't take my word for it, go to your local library and search through the stacks historical records.

I recommend that you do this sooner than later because microfiche files and dusty old reference books won't always be available in their original form. The days of burning books are far from over. Now that everything is being digitized online, the next wave of revisionist historians can easily modify any book that contradicts their narrative.

If you want another perspective, then sit down with a few elderly people in your area and ask for their perspectives on life. It's worth the small investment of time on your part. In the 1950s, newspapers wrote about big tent revivals and the miracles that accompanied those spectacular events. The published records contained testimonies from medical experts, Journalists, and other unbiased eyewitness reports.

There was a good deal of skepticism and unbelief in the papers, but even that was conducted better than it is today. Today's reporters can't be bothered to cover the Christian conferences or packed out stadium crusades, not unless they can find a reason to tarnish our reputation. Any reasonable person would want to tell their community (and read news reports about) a large, fun, peaceful public event, regardless of who sponsored the gathering.

We are in a war for control over information, it's an attack on the truth itself. Companies like Google, Facebook and Amazon have far more power than we'd like to believe.

If you've followed the progression, or rather regression, of leadings websites like Wikipedia over the years, you can see how the narrative has been skillfully slanted and distorted.

Nonprofits like this are given automatic credibility and the assumption of neutrality. They usually begin with noble intentions, but somewhere along the way, the waters become muddied and objectivity flies out the window right along with personal integrity. I realize that history cannot be taught without any opinions added into the mix, but what's happening now is widespread, intentional misinformation and slander. History books are being weaponized and white-washed by wealthy, powerful God haters.

Every inch of ground is hotly contested I this war is real, and living in denial will only cost you more territory in the long run. Opinions are presented as facts by our adversary the devil, who is the father of lies. (John 8:44) The hordes of hell are marching against the church and every voice matters in this ideological war over worldviews.

There are plenty of ways to use your voice to defeat the lies of the enemy. You could start a video blog and write articles for your local newspaper. Let your light shine, and speak the truth in love. It doesn't have to be perfectly scripted or professionally produced. Do a podcast if you're camera-shy or write a blog that later becomes a book. Do something, anything, and partner with friends who are gifted in areas where you are not strong.

Keep pushing forward, little by little. The gatekeepers of entertainment and media may be giants, but you are not a grasshopper. (Numbers 13:33) Remember the faith of Joshua and Caleb, who were brave when everyone else was afraid! Today you might feel weak, but in our weakness, He is made strong. At the same time, strength comes from putting your hand to the plow. You can be successful in your sphere of influence because God has called you there and He is faithful. "Do you see someone skilled in their work? They will serve before kings; they will not serve before officials of low rank." -Proverbs 22:29 NIV

Chapter 19

Idle Idols
or
Willing spirit - Weak body

"Our people must learn to devote themselves to doing what is good, in order to provide for urgent needs and not live unproductive lives." -Titus 3:14 NIV

"The safest road to hell is the gradual one-the gentle slope, soft underfoot, without sudden turnings, without milestones, without signposts." - C.S. Lewis

What you say about yourself is an opinion, what other people say is your reputation. Good intentions are one thing, but your track record is another altogether. We know that love keeps no record of wrong, and love covers a multitude of sins, but it always seems like cultural Christians twist

Bible verses about grace into excuses for inactivity and early retirement.

Do you take action like the good samaritan when disaster strikes? Are you filled with love, joy, peace, patience, kindness, gentleness and self-control? We all have bad days, but we do consistently, day in and day out is plain to see. Bearing good fruit isn't just your best moments, it has to do with your "standard operating procedure" and how you handle stressful situations. When it comes to resolving conflicts, what would your neighbors or co-workers say about your behavior?

Soliciting feedback from others is the best and easiest way to find blind spots. Are you prone to outbursts of angry? Rage is a highly addictive idol. Are you the calmest person in the room? That's great, but false humility and a critical spirit can leave you feeling just as defiled as wrath. Spiritual growth requires far more than self help, but it's good to have a practical to-do list. We can't be perfected by the flesh, (Galatians 3:3) but it's still important to crucify our flesh. (Galatians 5:24)

Sports can become an idol, and we touched on that earlier in this book. Even so, the lessons we learn from games, practice, and teamwork are extremely important. Some of the most effective soul winners today are professional athletes, retired coaches, and military Veterans. I believe that certain life lessons can only be learned by repeatedly facing difficult, competitive challenges.

If your success in athletics has made you popular, it's only natural that others will look up to you. That's a great opportunity to give God the glory. The harvest is ripe, and there's plenty of opportunities to share your faith on football fields, basketball courts, and golf courses. Even if you're a chess champion, your talent is an open door that cannot be ignored. Don't minimize or downplay your potential because it's a gift from God.

A few years ago I met a retired coach at a church

conference who said he always wanted to go on an overseas mission trip. During a lunch break, we sat down to talk. He shared his heart and how he felt guilty about avoiding mission trips for so long. He claimed to be so busy that even a part-time ministry commitment was unthinkable.

As if on cue, his wife walked up and caught the tail end of our conversation. She said; "if my husband stopped watching TV all day he'd have plenty of time for me and the ministry." The retired coach's face turned red, but he didn't object because he knew she was right.

By the time we parted ways, it was clear that he was healthy, well educated and willfully choosing to waste his golden years. I hope he went home, sold his TV, and used the proceeds to put a downpayment on a mission trip.

Everyone grows old, but age itself is not an indicator of maturity of wisdom. Mature Christians don't play the victim card or wait until they feel led. Passion for Jesus is the opposite of sitting around, waiting and hoping for someone to ask you to volunteer at their ministry. Those leaders are busy doing God's work, and I'm sure they would appreciate it if you took the first few steps by faith.

The history books in Heaven will be 100% honest about everyone and everything. A great example of a life well-lived is David Wilkerson. He was one of the most widely respected Christian leaders of his generation. In the late 1950s, when Wilkerson was a young pastor in a small town, he felt led by the Holy Spirit to sell his TV and dedicate an extra hour to prayer each day. By faith, he prayed for the young men who were members of violent gangs in New York City.

Before selling his TV, Wilkerson was only watching one hour of TV each day. Even so, after reading an article in a magazine about gang-related crime, he felt compelled to make a small sacrifice for the sake of strangers in another state. That decision radically changed the course of his life and countless others.

If David Wilkerson had ignored that little nudge, he could have enjoyed a pleasant life as a small-town pastor, but that was not his highest purpose and calling. Living a life that's good enough is reasonable and even admirable to some, but Wilkerson's decision led to the salvation of dangerous criminals and thousands of underprivileged young people. Many lives were transformed and ministries were birthed from Wilkerson's imitation of Christ.

David Wilkerson didn't care about fame, his wanted to stay on the narrow path and honor God. As a direct result of that obedience, Wilkerson's ministry Teen Challenge and World Challenge are still bearing fruit today. Now that I'm married with kids there are days when I only have one or two hours of free time. I think we should all give God the first and last hour of each day.

If you've never stuck with a devotional time before, start with half an hour or fifteen minutes. If that's all you can handle at first, that's OK. Stick with it and slowly build up to a full hour. Silence your phone, turn off the TV and you'll sleep better as a direct result. Read the Bible on your lunch break and listen to an audio Bible in your car. Make small changes like this and you'll experience a whole new level of peace during difficult times. "Everything is permissible for me," but not everything is beneficial. "Everything is permissible for me," but I will not be mastered by anything." -1 Corinthians 6:12 BSB

The athlete who trains with twenty-pound weights slowly adds more weight and higher reps to grow stronger. The same is true for triathletes or marathon runners. It's not complicated, just forgive yourself when you fail and renew your commitment to take new ground. Move forward or you will slide backward and lose what you've gained, there's nothing in-between. People often say they would die for Jesus, but precious few are living for Him.

There's no one size fits all solution. Some of us are doing too much, others are doing too little. If you're part of a social group that's dragging you down and leading you astray, drop them like a bad habit. Find a group of solid believers who are running after Christ in such a way that inspires you to dig deeper. Be a big brother or sister and start making disciples (not just converts) just like Jesus.

"he will go before him in the spirit and power of Elijah, to turn the hearts of the fathers to the children, and the disobedient to the wisdom of the just, to make ready for the Lord a people prepared."
-Luke 1:17 ESV

"When you are in the final days of your life, what will you want? Will you hug that college degree in the walnut frame. Will you ask to be carried to the garage so you can sit in your car? Will you find comfort in reading your financial statement? Of course not. What will matter then will be people. If relationships will matter most then, shouldn't they matter most now?" -Max Lucado

Years ago, when I was in high school, a science teacher asked our class to select any object in the room, and identify whether it was growing, decaying, or idling. As we suggested various items that appeared to be idle, we quickly learned our lesson; everything that wasn't growing (like a person or a plant) was in a slow process of decay.

As a group, we failed to find anything that wasn't growing or dying. The concept of idling, as we understood it, was a fallacy. A better example of idling would be a car that burns a little fuel as the engine runs, even though it remains stationary. An idle car isn't going anywhere, but it's internal components are gradually wearing down. "Teach us to number our days, that we may gain a heart of wisdom." -Psalm 90:12 NIV

Rest is important as we struggle against the inevitable effects of decay, and practicing stillness is an important skill that can be difficult. We can't run around all the time and treat our bodies like machines. On the other end of the spectrum, there's a counterfeit of God's Psalm 23 stillness and rest for the weary.

When some of us read about resting in the Lord or living by faith, we make a quantum leap of logic and choose to ignore the parts of the Bible that teach about, and commend hard work. The choice to live an idle life isn't Biblical, and that's true even if super-spiritual Christians claim otherwise. Anyone can pray, fast, and worship while they work.

What about full-time ministers who don't work at a church or a charitable organization? God didn't call anyone to be unaccountable to authority, but that doesn't mean your full-time ministry has to look like a typical denomination. At the International House of prayer, there are hundreds of missionaries who find creative ways to raise support and work odd jobs just to keep going. Intercessory prayer warriors and full-time musicians are often accused of being idle, but that isn't true.

I think we've all met someone who's lazy and pretends to be in full-time ministry, but that doesn't mean every freelance evangelist or independent missionary is a bum. What's the difference between work and play? It's hard to judge without evidence, so don't be quick to condemn. Looks can be deceiving and there are plenty of ministers who are content to live a quiet life and don't boast about their accomplishments.

"Be careful not to practice your righteousness in front of others to be seen by them. If you do, you will have no reward from your Father in heaven. "So when you give to the needy, do not announce it with trumpets, as the hypocrites do in the synagogues and on the streets, to be honored by others. Truly I tell you, they have received their reward in full. But when you give to the needy, do not let your left hand know what your right hand is doing, so that your giving may be in secret. Then your Father, who sees what is done in secret, will reward you." -Matthew 6:1-4 NIV

An obedient lifestyle leads us to work and rest at the right time. Jesus said we are either for Him or against Him, (Matthew 12:30) but Jesus also said, "Do not stop him, for no one who does a mighty work in my name will be able soon afterward to speak evil of me. For the one who is not against us is for us." -Mark 9:39,40 ESV

There is a balance to be articulated here, so sometimes it's better to mind your own business. If you prefer to donate to certain ministries that meet your high standards, that's great, but gossip and slander against other ministries is unacceptable. When you stop growing, you start dying. The speed of decay is much worse for those who refuse to learn new skills. It might take years to notice the decline, and it might take decades to feel the effects of your deficiencies. By that point, the damage is done, and it will considerably harder to rebuild what you've lost.

Life is full of seemingly idle moments when you're standing in line at the grocery store or sitting in the waiting room at the doctor's office. Those are perfect places for prayer, intercession, supplication, and giving thanks. Every new person you meet is an opportunity to share your faith.

Rush hour traffic grinds you down to a dead stop but that's a fast track to spiritual growth. Instead of getting upset, treat it like a mini-fast from driving. If you travel for work, you can listen to an audio Bible in 60-70 hours. For long distance commuters that can be accomplished in 2-3 months or less.

Do you believe in the power of prayer? Your commitment to prayer is tested every time the insurance company places you on hold for twenty minutes. Will you use that time to pray, or will you allow yourself to become frustrated, and then defile yourself by snapping at the customer support representative?

The harvest is ripe, but the intercessors are few. If you're stuck in a long line, there's nothing wrong with chatting up the people standing next to you. Your parents said don't talk to strangers, and that's good advice for elementary school students. If you're an adult it's time to put those childish ways behind you and grow up. Be prepared to share your testimony, in season and out of season, whenever the opportunity presents itself.

Who knows, you might be that person's only source of encouragement at just the right moment. An old musician once told me that he had forgotten more music than he remembered, and as brilliant as he was, I knew this was not hyperbole or false humility. He was one of the best, and that wasn't a matter of natural talent. It was a result of discipline, daily practice, a zeal for travel, a love for people, and a desire to learn new songs.

Everyone is growing older, but you don't have to become old and useless. One day you're a teenager with unlimited energy, and before you know it, you're raising teenagers and then grandkids. It's never too late to brighten up the last few chapters of your story. Years of idleness are far more harmful than years of hard labor, and the phrase "use it or lose it" isn't a cliché, it's a fact. "For to the one who has, more will be given, and he will have an abundance, but from the one who has not, even what he has will be taken away." -Matthew 13:12 ESV

Stay sharp and be on your guard, the people who look up to you will follow in your footsteps even when you tell them to follow Christ. Does your life resemble a mighty oak tree planted by a river, (Psalm 1) or is your life more like a wave of the sea, blown and tossed by the wind? (James 1:6) Rest when you need it, but remember, there's no neutral gear in life. Every day you will either take new ground or lose another small piece of what you've been given. Oh Lord, expand my territory, just like the prayer of Jabez! (1

Chronicles ch 4)

Chapter 20

Sloth and Gluttony

"You have lived on earth in luxury and self-indulgence. You have fattened yourselves in the day of slaughter." -James 5:5 NIV

"According to the most recent data, adult obesity rates now exceed 35 percent in four states, 30 percent in 25 states and are above 20 percent in all states... [meanwhile] More than 15 million U.S. children live in "food-insecure" households — having limited access to adequate food and nutrition due to cost, proximity and/or other resources." -stateofobesity.org

Pop quiz: What are two important Biblical terms that I've never heard in a sermon? Sloth and Gluttony. Why are these deadly sins omitted from nearly everyone's topical sermon series? We will explore that mystery in this chapter, but I think you can venture a guess without my help.

Different sins may be equal in God's eyes, (James

2:10) but the natural consequences of certain sins are anything but equitable. Laziness and obesity are seductive idols that are actively avoided by preachers, and I hope this book will help change that unfortunate trend. I had to search online to find a sermon series on both subjects, and the best ones were usually associated with network marketing companies, not churches.

I'm in good shape now but I've struggled with my weight in the past. Whenever I speak about health and fitness, I invariably meet skeptical overweight folks who automatically assume I've had an easy time achieving my results. These folks wouldn't want anyone to assume the worst about their issues, and yet they make negative assumptions about me because that's easier than facing the facts. When you've been judged harshly over your physical appearance, it's hard to avoid falling for the same critical spirit.

Pastors are good at keeping the peace, and I admire their ability to maintain unity. They don't want to alienate anyone, maybe that's one reason they invite guest speakers like me to shake things up once in a while. I don't want to be the bearer of bad news, but at least we know the solution is always the Good News. God deserves the glory for every victory, and our testimony has the power to inspire others. If someone is offended by my boldness, it usually has little to do with me and more to do with their hangups.

I think it's time for every leader to preach repentance and speak out against the seven deadly sins. Silence in the face of evil isn't love, it's complicity. I'm certainly no Dietrich Bonhoeffer, but obesity is now the leading cause of death in America, according to the New York Times. No matter how loving you are, it's still politically incorrect to preach against gluttony, but the Holy Spirit gives us the grace to handle touchy subjects.

In my opinion, most people don't care enough to confront your issues. The clinical word obesity is used to describe someone who has moved beyond being a bit overweight or full-figured. Some of us are naturally larger than others, and it's OK to be full-figured, but obesity is deadly. Just to be clear, body shaming has nothing to do with what I'm discussing in this book. Even encouragement can feel like condemnation to a calloused heart, but it's time to break up that fallow ground.

This chapter isn't about dogs, but before we address the plank or speck in our eye, I feel compelled to ask, are your dogs and cats overweight? It should be embarrassing to admit that when millions of American children (and billions worldwide) are living in 'food-insecure' households. Do your animals overeat to the point that it hurts their health? If that's the case, it would be wise to reconsider the decisions that led to your current situation.

I was looking through a large collection of old photographs from the 1800s recently, and I couldn't help but notice the absence of obesity. After reviewing hundreds of black and white images, I found only a few photos with overweight adults and virtually none with overweight kids.

I hate to say it, but the heaviest people we're usually government officials or business owners who were posing in front of their butcher shop, restaurant or a grocery store. Context is key. None of the individuals in those antique albums was close to the level of obesity and morbid obesity that's common in church today. The definition of an average American life has drastically changed over the last century.

Life was harder back then and most careers involved at least some level of backbreaking work, but in a way, it was more fulfilling. Junk food was rare, soft drinks didn't exist, and only the wealthiest families could afford to opt-out of labor intensive, household chores.

Today, on the escalator of success, we're straining under the weight of our prosperity. Thanks to rapid advances in science and technology, we can make thousands of bad choices without feeling the consequences. Doctors give advice that's usually ignored and prescribe powerful pills or surgical procedures to treat preventable diseases. By the way, these ailments wouldn't be labeled as preventable if you couldn't change your situation.

Thanks to our medicine cabinet full of uppers and downers, we hardly feel the effects of guzzling endless buckets of soda or stuffing our faces with greasy, fast food. The most slothful and sedentary lifestyle will make you feel lethargic, sure, but that's tolerable as long as the medical professionals are willing to pump you full of steroids, hormones, and antibiotics.

Sick-care is mistaken for healthcare and society races toward the extreme limits of self-indulgence. The marvels of modern science can reduce our symptoms but nothing can supplement the natural high that comes from reaching our goals. The consequences of bad decisions are greatly delayed by modern medicine, but we can only put off the inevitable for so long.

At the risk of being too blunt, I think it's fair to say the consequences of sins like gluttony have been intentionally ignored and downplayed by overweight ministry leaders who could stand to lose some weight. The Bible takes it a step further in regards to carnal Christians, "Their end is destruction, their god is their belly, and they glory in their shame, with minds set on earthly things." - Philippians 3:19 ESV

I have been guilty of serving the "god of my belly" but I fear God now and will go out of my way to avoid that fatal mistake. The physical, mental, emotional and spiritual aspects of life are all closely connected. You could suffer from an injury or illness and still maintain an amazing spiritual life. However, by definition, there's no such thing as a glutton or a slothful person who's running after the Lord with all of his heart, soul, mind, and strength.

"Consecrate yourselves for tomorrow, and you shall eat meat, for you have wept in the hearing of the Lord, saying, "Who will give us meat to eat? For it was better for us in Egypt." Therefore the Lord will give you meat, and you shall eat. You shall not eat just one day, or two days, or five days, or ten days, or twenty days, but a whole month, until it comes out at your nostrils and becomes loathsome to you, because you have rejected the Lord..." -Numbers 11:18-20 ESV

"People who regularly attend church are more likely to be obese than those who do not regularly attend. I find this disturbing. It's not the simple fact that these people are obese in and of itself that is the issue. But the research clearly shows that obesity is linked to higher rates of mortality and other related diseases. Obesity in the United States is also a $179 billion burden on our economy."
-Dale Fletcher

Unchecked idolatry is a self-inflicted death sentence. That's a fact, and it's important to remember that unpleasant realities aren't proof that God is mean or vindictive. Consequences are the natural result of foolishness, and God generously gives wisdom to help us avoid unnecessary suffering.

The Lord has lovingly provided us with His Holy Spirit, His written Word and His body, which is the church. Sloth or gluttony may be the hardest battle you've ever faced, but this struggle is allowed to strengthen your spirit. You can't be a spiritual warrior without going to battle. You can't win every time, but we're all expected to get out of bed and fight the good fight.

Are you in the race to win, or are you trying to not lose? There's a world of difference between those two mindsets. What are you willing to risk for the Kingdom of God? Would you endure pain, discomfort, failure, or rejection? I'm sure you've faced those already, so why not keep going and run your race in such a way as to win the prize? "I discipline my body like an athlete, training it to do what it should. Otherwise, I fear that after preaching to others I myself might be disqualified." -1 Corinthians 9:27 NLT

The call to discipline your body and force it to obey your will is a Biblical mandate. It's not just a suggestion, it's the best advice you'll ever receive on this subject. Philosophers call it mind over matter. The Gospel has the power to set you free from the bondage of sin. Gluttony and sloth can be as bad as any drug addiction, and you won't find freedom until you stop making exceptions and excuses.

Have you ever met an obese person in their late 70's or 80's? Probably not, because they don't usually live that long. In most cases, the larger you are the earlier you'll die from preventable diseases.

It's sad to see obese five and six-year-old who waddle when they walk. At that age, it would be silly to blame the kids and not the parents.

Generational bondage is handed down from mother and daughter and father to son, but today is a good day to break those chains. The statistics are frightening for overweight children, and the fault rests solely on parents and guardians. Jesus gave a dire warning to those who would lead little ones astray, (Matthew 18:6) and that comparison is fair because gluttony is a deadly sin.

Little kids cannot become obese without enablers. Parents can't take all the blame as long as pastors sugar coat their sermons with the sweetest Bible verses while avoiding political subjects. Cotton candy ministers might pack the pews and fill up the offering plates, but it's an affront to God, and it leads to spiritual diabetes.

It's unbearable to watch a spiritually malnourished congregation drink their spiritual milk without being exposed to the weightiness of spiritual meat. Having faith like a little child is a virtue, and that's why the abuse of ministerial power is such a severe crime. That's why the Bible says; "Not many of you should become teachers, my fellow believers because you know that we who teach will be judged more strictly." -James 3:1 NIV

If preachers serve their congregation too many "high fructose corn syrup" sermons, (those are the sweetest messages without any difficult or challenging Bible verses), then we'll leave church each week with a bloated belly and a thirsty soul. (Psalm 63:1) When pastors teach on fasting, self-denial and crucifying the flesh, part of the congregation might walk away or accuse him of preaching works-based salvation. That's a risk you'll have to accept if you fear the Lord more than man.

Obesity is an outward symptom of unresolved trauma and gluttony can manifest itself in a variety of strange ways. Did you know the god of the stomach can be found in a person whose militant about organic food? Eating healthy isn't a problem when you're rich or if you live next to an organic farm. If you live in a big city, the cost of eating only 'farm fresh organics' could add thousands to your monthly budget. How will you maintain that posh diet if the Lord calls you to a long term mission in a remote African village?

I believe the same "god of stomach" idol is common among bodybuilders to eat upwards of 10,000 calories each day. That's enough food for five ordinary adults. Do you need to look like the Incredible Hulk just to win people for Jesus? I may not understand the appeal of being a professional weight lifter or a fitness model, but hey, if you have a clear conscience about spending six hours a day in the gym while holding down a full-time job and caring for a family, that's your choice.

It's between you and God, but I would encourage you to seek advice from pastors and other mature believers who don't have the same lifestyle as you. ""Everything is permissible for me," but not everything is beneficial. "Everything is permissible for me," but I will not be mastered by anything." -1 Corinthians 6:12 BSB

If you're extremely particular about gourmet food, or

if you've been known to make mealtime unpleasant for anyone who isn't gluten-free, then you have a high risk factor for idolatry. By now it should be clear that being a picky eater isn't a crime, but nearly anything can become an idol. This isn't a fault-finding mission it's about setting yourself from anything that hinders.

Emotional eaters find more comfort in food than Jesus, and that's a serious problem. The name of Jesus is above every name and disorder. His blessings and promises are sufficient for overcoming any curse. I believe the testimonies I've heard from women and men who have been set free from eating disorders through the power of the one true God who is love. Jesus can lead anyone to victory over bulimia and anorexia. As we draw near to Him we will begin to embrace our immense preciousness and beauty. "Let the king be enthralled by your beauty; honor him, for he is your lord." -Psalm 45:11 NIV

Some of us eat too much, others intentionally eat too little. I've met people who are hyper-focused on health food to the point of legalism, and others who pretend to be invincible and refuse to eat vegetables. I consider myself a foodie who enjoys cooking and trying new restaurants, which is fine, as long as that doesn't become an obsession. "For life is more than food, and the body more than clothing." -Luke 12:23 ESV

Please hear my heart on this because we're all prone to errors of extremes. I lost 30 pounds and 4.5 inches from my waist a few years ago and I've kept it off since then. I bought myself a used juice machine for Christmas and committed to a strict vegetable juice fast. I cheated on my diet a few times during the first two weeks, but I got back up and started over again. All I did was force my body to submit to my willpower.

My experience wasn't like a weight lifter pumping huge weights, but a marathon runner who trains himself to mentally endure many long miles. After a few ups and downs, I made it through 21 days on nothing but homemade juice, water, and green tea. It felt amazing to flood my body with fresh vitamins, minerals, and enzymes.

This juice fast increased my mental clarity, my mood improved and I started waking up earlier without an alarm clock. I lost my cravings for caffeine, sweets, salty snacks and alcohol. As crazy as it sounds, I started craving fresh fruits and veggies. That shift in my appetite made all the difference. Even today it's easier for me to walk past the potato chips and sweet treats at the grocery store.

My seasonal allergies were getting worse each year and they were unbearable when I started juicing, it was horrible. Thanks to a few, minor lifestyle changes, I don't need prescription allergy medication or steroid shots. Since then, I've done other fasts, including intermittent fasts and water only fasts.

Today, I'm not 100% consistent, but I have more than enough energy to go to the gym. I attribute much of my success to reading educational books and watching YouTube videos from real experts who aren't greedy little fad-diet phonies and con-artists. Here's the deal, no one can make a ton of money by telling you to consume only water until you feel better.

That's the big secret, and it works better than anything else I've tried. Hardly anyone promotes fasting (thankfully that's changing thanks to the Internet) because no one ever got rich by encouraging people to consume nothing. My mother had a juice machine when I was little, and she used to make us juice when I was growing up. Those fond memories were the main reason I gave juice a chance.

It may sound crazy or counter-intuitive, but God's path often involves dying to ourselves. Death to self is the surest path to storing up treasures in Heaven. I've said before, and it's worth saying again, most people will try anything other than the hardest thing. When this life is over, there will be no more secrets, and everything hidden will be revealed.

(Matthew 10:26) Even now we are "surrounded by a great cloud of witnesses" who are watching everything. (Hebrews 12:1)

That great cloud of witnesses, those are your biggest fans. Do you believe this, or are you still struggling with unbelief? All of Heaven is rooting for you, and hoping for the best. Today is the day to repent, to reconsider, to turn around and start living like children of the light. We want to believe it's more complicated, but this part is painfully simple. Dollars and cents, hours and minutes, calories in and calories out. That's not the whole story, but it's a huge part. What are you doing with all those talents? You've been given more than a few.

"Everyone who competes in the games trains with strict discipline. They do it for a crown that is perishable, but we do it for a crown that is imperishable. Therefore I do not run aimlessly; I do not fight like I am beating the air. No, I discipline my body and make it my slave, so that after I have preached to others, I myself will not be disqualified." -1 Corinthians 9:26 BSB

Chapter 21

Golden Idols

"As for the rich in this present age, charge them not to be haughty, nor to set their hopes on the uncertainty of riches, but on God, who richly provides us with everything to enjoy. They are to do good, to be rich in good works, to be generous and ready to share, thus storing up treasure for themselves as a good foundation for the future, so that they may take hold

of that which is truly life."
-1 Timothy 6:17-19 ESV

"Debt is probably the main reason why Christians today are not free to respond to the call of God in their lives. When there is a call to do anything, from entering the full-time ministry to going on a mission trip, if our main consideration is whether we can afford it, it is an indication that our financial condition rules us more than the will of God does. It is a revelation of just how much we have built our lives upon the foundations of this present age, rather than hearing and obeying the Word of the Lord." -Rick Joyner

What's the worst idol? It's anything that captures your heart. What's the most pervasive idol? Money, hands down, because that's what feeds most other idols. Some may object and call this guilt by association, but we're dealing with life as it is, not as we'd like it to be.

The gilded god of greed is a metaphor for money, power, control, and consumerism. It's no coincidence that Aaron forged his calf from gold. Do you trust God to supply your provisions? When we stop relying on our abilities to earn money and solicit donations, we can operate freely, without any manipulation. It's time to stop trying to carry the weight of the world on your shoulders. Cast your burdens upon the Lord and He will lighten your load.

When we embrace the fact that our primary ministry is to the Lord, and not busyness, we are then able to accomplish greater things without obsessing over efficiency or productivity. So many well-intended Christians are absolutely overwhelmed by the pursuit of riches and pleasure. Jesus said, "And as for what fell among the thorns, they are those who hear, but as they go on their way they are choked by the cares and riches and pleasures of life, and their fruit does not mature." -Luke 8:4-16 ESV

If your fruit does not mature, that means it's inedible. Have you ever tried to eat unripe fruit? It tastes terrible, causes indigestion, and can be toxic. Unripe fruit will give you a seriously painful stomach ache which isn't good for the body. At the end of this age, I don't want God to declare that my life's work wasn't good for the body of Christ. I want to be a fully mature believer.

Let's take a moment to consider the parable of the sower in Luke chapter 8. The seed is the word of God. When the seed is scattered among thorns, that represents the trappings of wealth. Have you ever stumbled into a thorn bush? It can happen in an instant, and before you know what's happened, you're tangled up in razor-sharp leaves and branches. It's easy to walk into the briars, but it's painful and difficult to pull yourself free from such a mess.

As we've learned from previous chapters, idolatry isn't complicated. When we're stuck in denial and pretend like our excuses are valid, we only fool ourselves. You might blame your parents or a spouse, but when it comes to idolatry, no puts a gun to your head. Greedy people become workaholics for various reasons, but when it plays out, it's always a rejection of God's plan.

The same is true for non-working, empty nest spouses who ignore the ministry and pursue a life of luxury and leisure. We have no control over our lot in life, but we are responsible for our attitude and actions. Like Joseph from the book of Genesis, you can thrive in any situation. We must learn to be content (not passive or complacent) regardless of our circumstances.

It's important to remember the definition of biblical prosperity stretches far beyond material possessions. If you claim to "prosper in all things and be in health, just as your soul prospers." -3 John 1:2 NKJV well, that's a bold claim indeed. That would mean your emotional, mental, physical, and spiritual life are just as phenomenal as your investment portfolio.

Rich people (and those who devote themselves to chasing wealth) are pierced with many sorrows as a direct result of over-emphasizing money. (1 Timothy 6:10) It's an idol whether you admit it or not. Being successful in business might make you popular, but God isn't impressed by your bank account. Generosity and selfless love are far more important.

The wages of sin is death, and greed destroys families just as surly as cigarettes destroy your heart and lungs. I've worked with dozens of rich men who told me about their severely dysfunctional lives. Their kids hated them, their wives resented them, and their business partners were treacherous. The worst ones firmly believed that their life was as good as they could reasonably expect.

These captains of industry were not prospering in all things, not by a long shot. Every good gift is from God, but money isn't a sign that God approves of your lifestyle. The same is true with leaders who oversee a successful ministry. Even if you grow a megachurch from a small Bible study, that isn't proof of God's approval. Some of us crave power and popularity more than cold, hard cash, but the love of money is still the root of all kinds of evil. (1 Timothy 6:10)

At the end of the day, it's foolish to rest on our past accomplishments because every day brings new challenges and deadly temptations. Jesus put it this way: "he makes his sun rise on the evil and on the good, and sends rain on the just and on the unjust." -Matthew 5:45 ESV

As a consultant, I've worked with thousands of wealthy individuals in places like Beverly Hills and Palm Beach. I've also spent time with thousands of poor people through charity work, church events, and mission trips. Based on what I've seen, I usually prefer the company of friends in low places. The poorest Christians tend to be happier than the rich ones. They are far more relaxed, content, and joyful. They love to serve the Lord and choose to walk by faith.

The generosity that I've witnessed among poor believers often reminds me of the widow's mite. (Mark 12:41-44) God cares about how much you give as it relates to your overall income. The total percent is important because God is fair and impartial. Career idolatry and the worship of wealth will lead you to believe that a rich man's endowment is more valuable than the widow's mite. That might be true is God was desperate for our help, but He doesn't need our help. We need His discipline.

"Those of low estate are but a breath; those of high estate are a delusion; in the balances they go up; they are together lighter than a breath." -Psalm 62:9 ESV

Before we continue, let's clear up a few rumors about money. First of all, money is not the central them of the Bible, not by far. I've seen that nonsense so many times online. It just won't go away. Money is not the main focus of any book in the Bible, and Jesus did not teach about money more than any other subject. Fortunately, a plain reading of the Bible speaks for itself if you are earnestly searching for the truth.

Don't take my word for it, read the Bible from cover to cover and take notes. Greedy little lies will always spread like wildfire online, but when you read the Bible often it's easier to spot false teaching. Jesus promised that His sheep would know His voice, but He also said that those on the narrow path would be few. Spiritually immature money worshippers cling to a handful of cherry-picked, out of context scriptures.

The prosperity preachers who make a career out of spreading misinformation cannot provide Biblical "line upon line, percept upon precept" (Isaiah 28:10) references to support their claims. Books like Proverbs and Deuteronomy each have several positive lines about financial prosperity, but then again, I've never met anyone who didn't understand the positive potential of a large bank account, nor have I met anyone who went out of their way to stay poor because it was the spiritual thing to do. I know it's possible, but I've never met one.

The most commonly misused verses in the Old Testament are cause and effect lessons about hard work, diligence, and righteousness. It's never an endorsement for anything close to materialism or consumerism. Most of the Bible verses that mention money sound like this one: "He who loves money will not be satisfied with money, nor he who loves wealth with his income; this also is vanity." - Ecclesiastes 5:10 ESV

Prosperity preachers will try to trick you into believing they are an authority on the issue, but most of them are hucksters. False prosperity advocates are usually gifted speakers, but the Kingdom of God is not a matter of mere words. I hate to say this but false teachers tend to be overconfident evangelists who refuse to stay in their lane. They would do well to stick with preaching the simple Gospel of faith, hope, love, and repentance.

Prosperity preachers love using big words and they're experts at impressing immature Christians who judge by outward appearances and those who lack discernment. If you're dead set on being greedy and want to find someone who will tell you what you want to hear, it's not hard in this day and age.

A steady diet of unbalanced, exaggerated, prosperity preaching has led to the proliferation of full-blown prosperity pimps. These are the byproduct and natural consequences of sowing and reaping. These (mostly) young men are like a photocopy of a photocopy, and the lowest standards of old-school prosperity preachers have become the highest standards of the next generation of prosperity pimps.

This embarrassing subset of Christianity feeds on a steady diet of inspirational tweets and Memes. Their message is a dumbed-down version of over-simplified and reductive sermons. What they teach is little more than a list of shallow sound bites strung together in a row. What's worse is that these are passionate (albeit misguided) believers who love the Lord enough to do something.

People like this conduct most of their so-called ministry work online, as keyboard warriors. They create a barrier around themselves to avoid anyone who isn't loyal to their cult of personality. When they aren't basking in the praise of their fans, the most successful ones prefer to hide out in church green rooms as they actively avoid mixing with ordinary folks. They block and ban anyone who doesn't gobble up what they're selling, but it's harder to get rid of someone in person than it is online.

The worst ones are wolves in sheep's clothing, but I don't want to call preachers out by name because condemnation isn't my job. God knows who they are, and I have my suspicions, but if we aren't praying for our enemies, then we need to start right now.

Sunday offerings are collected from mostly single mothers, struggling families, and elderly folks on a fixed income. When prosperity preachers are involved, those charitable donations are extracted through empty promises. Then, God's storehouse is plundered by men and women who selfishly squander donations on expensive clothes, luxury cars, luxury homes, and five star hotels.

Beloved, it's OK to buy nice things with the money you've earned, but donations are not earned, they're a gift given unto the Lord. It's evil to use tithes and offerings for selfish gain. What' the first Beatitude? "And he lifted up his eyes on his disciples, and said: "Blessed are you who are poor, for yours is the kingdom of God." -Luke 6:20 ESV

If you have the chance to question a prosperity preacher in person, they will try to charm you with their charisma. If a little flattery doesn't shut you up, they usually try to make a quick exit or, if cornered, assert themselves as the dominant, alpha male. If the schoolyard bully routine fails to keep anyone in line, they will dismissively shun the questioner. For good measures, they typically accuse the questioner of being mean spirited and divisive.

"Therefore an overseer must be above reproach... not a lover of money." -1 Timothy 3:2,3 ESV

All opinions aside, personal finance is a critical issue, so don't get it twisted. Thankfully, a plain reading of scripture leaves little room for misinterpretation. It's hard to miss what Jesus says about money unless you're going out of your way to justify greed. Anyone can easily pick up the obvious truth when you abandon all those conceited, self-centered, and vain ambitions.

The Bible provides many direct warnings against the kind of greed that's subtly preached today in the name of Jesus. Widespread deception, even among leaders, is just another sign of the times. Some Christians do suffer from a spirit of poverty, which is wrong, but one extreme doesn't justify the other.

Anyone who claims Jesus was overly positive about money certainly didn't get that insight from the Bible, they got it secondhand from popular preachers. When a pastor prattles on about money, the donations are typically larger. Everyone knows that but it's not the pastor's job to prime the pumps or emotionally manipulate a congregation.

In less than five minutes anyone can search through a Bible concordance or commentary. There are plenty of helpful, easily searchable websites like BibleHub.com and OpenBible.info which both provide more resources than anyone could absorb in a lifetime. Reading a bit of research isn't hard, and it doesn't take much effort.

With all that in mind, I should say that money isn't evil and, wealthy people aren't any better or worse than you. Most of us would benefit from reading a Dave Ramsey book once in a while. At the end of the day, it's helpful to be mindful of the fact that Godliness with contentment is great gain. "Keep your life free from love of money, and be content with what you have, for he has said, "I will never leave you nor forsake you." -Hebrews 13:4 ESV

Why does Jesus mention money in over a dozen parables? Hard work, generosity, and eternal judgment are easy to understand through the context of money and real estate transactions because humans are earthly minded. Jesus is willing to work with us in our current condition, no matter how desperate. The Kingdom of God can be easily explained to princes and paupers with the help of financial 'cause and effect' illustrations.

Like it or not, money is the primary measuring stick in the secular world. That's why everyone can relate to stories that involve money. The parables of Christ are not centered on money, instead, they are centered on Christ. Money is a useful tool, but it's only a means to an end. Will you sow some of that seed or will you greedily eat it all? Our attitude towards money reveals the condition of our hearts. Jesus said, "You cannot serve God and money." -Matthew 6:24 ESV

Beloved, I've been to numerous churches that feature a mini-sermon on money every Sunday. That isn't God's will, it's manipulation for the sake of greed. Each week enterprising pastors invent new ways of working their congregation up into a feeding frenzy before the offering plates are passed around. "These people honor me with their lips, but their hearts are far from me. They worship me in vain; their teachings are merely human rules." -Matthew 15:8,9 NIV

Prosperity pastors, elders, deacons, and their guest speakers love to dress up prettier than their wives and they take turns trying to out do each other with outlandish claims about things that Jesus never said. In certain denominations the sin of greed is preached non-stop, and this has caused millions of Christians to walk away from organized religion. Every leader will be held responsible for every soul that's led astray or discouraged by reckless preaching.

"Jesus looked around and said to his disciples, "How difficult it will be for those who have wealth to enter the kingdom of God!" And the disciples were amazed at his words. But Jesus said to them again, "Children, how difficult it is to enter the kingdom of God! It is easier for a camel to go through the eye of a needle than for a rich person to enter the kingdom of God." -Mark 10:23-27 ESV

"Some theorize that the needle Jesus was speaking of was the Needle Gate, supposedly a low and narrow after-hours entrance found in the wall surrounding Jerusalem. It was purposely small for security reasons, and a camel could only go through it by stripping off any saddles or packs and crawling through on its knees. The problem with this theory is there is no evidence such a gate ever existed. Beyond that, what sane camel driver would go through such contortions when larger gates were easily accessible?" -GotQuestions.org

"The idea that the eye of a needle, referred to here, was a small gate through which a camel could enter only on his knees is without warrant. "The word for needle [in Greek] refers specifically to a sewing needle. Furthermore, Jesus was not talking about what man considers possible, but about what seems to be impossible..." -The Wycliffe Bible Commentary

I've seen prosperity preachers tap-dance around the facts of the "eye of the needle" story better than Bill "Bojangles" Robinson. The Bible is naturally antithetical to greedy preaching, and that's why prosperity advocates spend most of their time drawing their inspiration from extra-biblical sources, which is the case with most heretics. They hear a sermon from one of their buddies, and they borrow it without stopping for five minutes to check the facts.

When a fanciful story comes around, (the one about bowing low at the Eye of The Needle Gate) any pastor who is desperate for justification gets hit with a confirmation bias that's hard to resist. At this point, fact-checking your friends feels almost unspiritual and disloyal. Instead of being diligent, prosperity preachers take these old wives tales by faith and gleefully spin a yarn about some dubious Needle Gate in Jerusalem.

As the story goes, all you need to do is bow down low and temporarily unload your cargo. Then you can pass under the eye of the needle. Never mind the fact that Jesus said: "with man this is impossible". Important details like this are ignored for the sake of a extra-biblical story that bolsters their preconceived assumptions.

Let's take this silly story to its logical conclusion and see if it adds up. After all, it's true that rich people need to unload their metaphorical baggage. Don't we all? If you're still keeping score it's fair to assume the next step would be loading your cargo back onto the camel. Loading and unloading cargo? That's a far cry from impossible, and this man-made story is only helpful for confusing or downplaying God's clear warning about wealth.

If this superfluous supplement to the Gospel was true, which it isn't, the only takeaway would be that rich people can enter the Kingdom of God with a cute little bow or a curtsy. No need to repent or change your ways. This so-called 'special insight' that originated from overly ambitious prosperity preachers directly contradicts Jesus. Remember, it was the Pharisees who nullified God's Word for the sake of their traditions.

Was the Needle Gate real or fictional? It doesn't matter because that's beside the point. Jesus made frequent use of hyperbole to make His lessons more memorable. (20) There's no need to soften the blow or minimize His words.

The camel and sewing needle analogy is intentionally outlandish.

It's easier for a camel? That's called humor and it's an effective method of communication. Jesus never make mistakes, and all of His parables were designed to make a memorable, emotional impact. When Jesus said it's impossible for a rich person to enter the Kingdom of Heaven, He meant exactly what He said. He made the lesson funny because He is a real man with a real personality and humor makes the story stick with us. When the Word became flesh, it was never intended to be boring, dry, or dull.

This comedic exaggeration highlights the absurdity of anyone who thinks they can spoil themselves (or their dogs) rotten while others starve. (1 Corinthians 11:21) Christians who live in luxury believe God approves of their lifestyle, almost as if He was a pushover. Their actions prove that they don't believe God is fair or impartial.

Their life experience has taught them that money opens all kinds of doors and affords a wide variety of special privileges. If wealth is a sign of God's approval and favor, then why wouldn't God give them a little break on Judgment day? People never say this kind of stuff out loud, but these are the unspoken assumptions that guide their decisions.

"But Peter said to him, "May your silver perish with you, because you thought you could obtain the gift of God with money!" -Acts 8:20 ESV

Before we move on, let's take a moment to clarify the legitimate meaning of the camel and needle analogy. The takeaway is simple; "with God, all things are possible." (Matthew 19:26) In summary; difficult does not equal impossible, and if it's impossible, that means your money can't save you. Everyone needs to repent and turn from their wicked ways.

When in doubt, stick with what's written in the Bible.

When someone who wants to grow their fanbase shares a direct quote from the Bible, his or her followers won't automatically view that as unique or special, but it makes God happy. If you're always striving to be edgy or to say something new, in a way that it hasn't been said before, then it's wise to take a step back and question your motives. Who are you trying to promote? Jesus, or yourself?

Prosperity preachers go out of their way to coin new phrases and desperately try to make the Bible say something it never said. Those jokers could win an Academy Award for their acting skills, but I think Jesus was serious when He told the rich young ruler to sell everything and follow Him. It's hard to understand how that could that straight-forward line be misinterpreted apart from willful deceit.

What if the Lord visited you in a dream tonight, and asked you to sell your possessions and give the money away? I've seen leaders turn red in the face at the suggestion that God still wants us to be willing to lay it all down. If you felt strongly that God was calling you to give your possessions away to the poor, what would you do?

That's what plenty of missionaries do when they move to foreign mission fields. They pack up a couple of old suitcases and place their lives in God's hands. That level of commitment is almost unthinkable for anyone with a mountain of student loans, credit cards, mortgages, and car payments.

In my opinion, there's nothing wrong with using debt to buy a home or start a business, (sorry Dave Ramsey) but many of us have gotten out of control with consumer debt.

We want our peers to view us as prosperous, but if you needed a car and you had to pay cash, what kind of car would you buy today? If you couldn't get a home loan and had to pay for the building materials and laborers out of pocket, how big would your new home be?

While we're on the subject of frugality, I've heard a lot of ridiculous, fearful myths about driving older cars.

Some say it's dangerous and foolhardy to buy a used car. These are people who go deep into debt for a new every two or three years. They tell themselves it's the only reasonable choice and everyone who works at the local car dealership agrees wholeheartedly.

I've never had a new car, not by a long shot. However, the used vehicles I've owned have always been reliable and comfortable. If that isn't enough, I'll let you in on a little secret; I don't repair or service my cars much at all. I mostly hire a mechanic, and it's no big deal. We're all entitled to our opinions, but you're flat out wrong if you say your family can't rely on a ten-year-old car.

I put tons of miles on my vehicles for work, and I've saved a ton of money buying cars that were at least four or five years old. Older vehicles might hurt your ego, but auto insurance is cheaper, and the monthly payments are lower. Buying a good used car will save you hundreds of dollars each month and that's true even when you factor in the cost of repairs.

People who can't quite afford a new car (but they do it anyways) frequently pick out the cheapest economy car on the dealer's lot. Those are generally compact, entry-level cars that tend to be unsafe and junky. They have terrible handling, weak acceleration, and a stiff ride. They aren't built to last and you can be sure that corners were cut to hit that low price point. If that's all you can afford, it's better to buy a mid-range used car and enjoy the improved performance and durability. If money is tight, buy a used car, keep it for a long time, and stay on top of the maintenance.

I don't buy used underwear or socks, but when it comes to big items, like furniture and musical instruments, I try to find one that's used before I consider buying something new. In the long run, it's better to pick quality over quantity. If you're willing to shop around and take your time, you can find great deals in the scratch and dent section, or by purchasing open item electronics with extended warranties.

What does shopping have to do with faith? The lessons we learn as we grow in patience and diligence are worth the inconvenience. Christians are supposed to be shrewd, but most of us have started to behave like pew potatoes who aren't very resourceful. It's time to step into a higher level of accountability and responsibility. The end times are going to be harsh, so gird up your loins, raise your standards, and prepare for the worst.

You will need to be careful when you're shopping in secondhand stores, garage sales, and online auctions. They are not like a department stores with an excellent return policy, but once you get the hang of it, it's fun. If you ask around, you've probably got a bargain hunter in your family who would be happy to help you.

What I'm saying is, you don't have to become a monk to earn God's favor, but then again, where would we be without the heroic and sacrificial lives of Martin Luther and Thomas à Kempis? God knows I've struggled with a desire for material possessions over the years, but I don't let that rule my life. I enjoy going to car shows once in a while to look at classic hot rods and futuristic concept cars.

I've always wanted a classic Porsche, and I hope that dream comes true someday, but I'll be OK if that doesn't happen. I'm still fairly young, but I could easily fill a book with stories about the many blessings that God has allowed me to experience for free.

What I have in Jesus is more than enough, and I can honestly say that I am satisfied with my portion. He provides for my wants and needs in incredible ways. The Lord has never failed to bless me in wonderful ways at just the right time. If He wants me to drive a sports car, He can make it happen.

"Find out how much God has given you and from it take what you need; the remainder is needed by others." – Saint Augustine

"God said to him, 'You fool! This very night your life will be demanded from you. Then who will get what you have prepared for yourself?' "This is how it will be with whoever stores up things for themselves but is not rich toward God." - Luke 12:20-21 NIV

If you're unhappy with your lot in life, it's time to search your heart and be honest. Are you praying for self-control as earnestly as you pray for financial blessings? How about hospitality and generosity, are you praying for an increase in those areas as much as you pray for success in business? "But seek first His kingdom and His righteousness, and all these things will be added to you. -Matthew 6:33 NASB

Why would God give you more if you aren't faithful in your current situation? How much do you invest in the Kingdom after your bills are paid each month? Now, how much goes toward hobbies, pleasure, and recreation? Do the math and look at the numbers side by side. Take a long hard look in the mirror and ask yourself; are my dreams and aspirations aligned with God's will?

I'm guilty of selfish ambitions at times, but when I submit those thoughts to the Lord He deals with my motives and helps me let go of everything that hinders. "You lust and do not have; so you commit murder. You are envious and cannot obtain; so you fight and quarrel. You do not have because you do not ask. You ask and do not receive, because you ask with wrong motives, so that you may spend it on your pleasures." -James 4:2-3 NIV

"Individuals and societies who devote themselves to money soon become devoured by it. Or, as the Bible reiterates, we become what we worship. Money almost literally seems to eat people away, drying up the sap of their vitality and withering their spontaneity, generosity and joy." -Os

The idol of money, also known as mammon, is deceitful above all else. The trouble with deception is that you don't know you've been deceived. When the good times are rolling, and money is flowing, we tend to believe our thoughts and goals are approved by God. We know that Abraham, David, and Solomon were rich, but a king's lifestyle isn't something you can name and claim.

The good Lord has blessed people with wealth, but we are living an age of unprecedented wealth. Even if you're a millionaire who spends money like a billionaire, you can always find someone with worse habits, and justify your actions by comparison. That's the kind of deception that makes greed difficult to root out.

Unscrupulous preachers love to misuse this verse; "For you know the grace of our Lord Jesus Christ, that though He was rich, yet for your sake He became poor, so that you through His poverty might become rich." -2 Corinthians 8:9 NASB

If you take the time to read a few commentaries about this verse, the consensus is clear. The Apostle Paul wasn't talking about material wealth, but spiritual rewards and treasures in Heaven. Our society worships the rich and famous, but God is no respecter of persons. His ways are higher than our ways. (Isaiah 55:8) Jesus can move mountains in your life without depositing a fat stack of cash in your bank account.

Nearly everyone who can read this book (or buy it but never find time to read it) is rich when compared to all of human history. How does your lifestyle stack up against the rest of the world? Do you have access to computers, schools, and a pubic library? Were you taught to read, write and solve math problems by qualified teachers? Do you have access to reliable transportation? How about warm clothes, shoes, and a home with a locking door?

Billions of humans would give anything to inherit your first world problems, and that's a fact. We are rich with opportunities, career potential, and free or low-cost educational resources. If anyone chooses to be wasteful or foolish with money that won't exempt us from the responsibility that goes along with our potential for great wealth. It's the parable of ten talents.

You might not have a dream job; but that's a temporary setback, that isn't abject poverty. Most Westerners are outrageously rich from a historical perspective. If you've ever visited a third world country then you know what I'm talking about. For now, it's sufficient to say, if you have access to what most of us take for granted, then you are extremely fortunate. Most of us have won the lottery depending on where you were born. Don't take it granted any longer. Instead, run your race with endurance.

"But those who want to get rich fall into temptation and a snare and many foolish and harmful desires which plunge men into ruin and destruction." -1 Timothy 6:9 NASB

In the past, I struggled with the story in Luke about the man who wanted to tear down his barns and build bigger ones. (Luke 12:13-21) His idea sounded reasonable to me, but it's clear from the story that Christ alone understood the intentions of his heart. Let's stop and think about it, this farmer decides to tear down his barns (we can assume his old barns were good enough). Now he wants to build larger barns in their place.

There's nothing wrong with growing a successful business, but that isn't the premise of this story. We can safely assume this wasn't as a business owner with a passion for creating jobs, but rather an individual with selfish motives. This isn't the same as Joseph who stored up grain in Egypt. Joseph was thrust into his position and remained faithful to his mandate from the Lord. (Genesis 41)

I think it would be wasteful to tear down one perfect good barn, let alone multiple barns. Can you imagine how much effort would go into building large barns by hand, thousands of years ago, all without power tools? That project would cost a fortune in today's dollars. Our ambitious farmer wanted to start from scratch, and all this effort just to add more cushion to an already impressive nest egg.

In context, we know he was operating outside of God's will, that's implied. The Gospels are short books, and when it comes to short stories, there isn't room for waste. Every detail is important and meaningful. As I seek the Lord to help me become more frugal, I can see this as a warning against greed, arrogance, the pride of life, self-reliance, and self-sufficiency.

How much do you need to stack up before shifting your focus to more charitable causes? The most common answer to that question, even if you ask a multi-millionaire, is likely to be 'just a little bit more." If you've had a successful career, and feel led to dedicate more time to ministry, why would you want to tear down your barns and build bigger ones? God often increases the cash flow of ministries according to their needs, as they grow. That's seed for the sower.

Why do so many Christians idolize wealth and ignore what the Bible says? "Keep your life free from love of money, and be content with what you have, for he has said, "I will never leave you nor forsake you." -Hebrews 13:5 ESV

Some of us seek pleasure, others want to avoid pain, but the love of money offers a false sense of security and he who is led astray by it is not wise. "Some trust in chariots and some in horses, but we trust in the name of the LORD our God." -Psalm 20:7 ESV

Interesting fact; the word retirement does not appear in the Bible, or other ancient Christian books because no one ever dreamed that they would be able to cease working entirely and move to Florida to play golf or sit by the beach every day. Our ancestors never dreamed of a pension, and history shows us that even kings generally worked themselves to death.

If you can live on a retirement income, I think you should view that as an open door for full-time ministry. Righteous retirement is best defined as a strategic transition from your previous role to an advisory role that's less physically demanding. I don't believe God calls anyone to fully retire, certainly not if your definition of retirement is full-time recreation with occasional church attendance.

Faithful watchmen make sensible adjustments and adaptations as they grow older, but they don't abandon their assignment. I think the best example of Biblical retirement is King David, who had to be pulled away from the battle by younger warriors. Surely he was a man after God's own heart. David's men admired his courage, but some jobs are for young men. At a certain point, it was no longer appropriate for the aging king of Israel to swing a sword. David's experience and wisdom were needed elsewhere.

"Once again there was a battle between the Philistines and Israel. David went down with his men to fight against the Philistines, and he became exhausted... But Abishai son of Zeruiah came to David's rescue; he struck the Philistine down and killed him. Then David's men swore to him, saying, "Never again will you go out with us to battle, so that the lamp of Israel will not be extinguished." -2 Samuel 21:15-17 NIV

"If you cannot mold yourself entirely as you would wish, how can you expect other people to be entirely to your liking?" - Thomas a Kempis

Don't let your lamp burn out, instead, ask God for the strength to rekindle the fire of your youth. I often wonder, how many aging congregations have failed to pass the torch to younger generations? It's easy to play the blame game, but how many thousands of churches have closed permanently after their aging leaders have failed to develop young leaders who can take over for elderly pastors?

If church leaders want to maintain a strict top-down management style, then it's fair to say the buck stops at the senior pastor and the elders. "Wake up, and strengthen what remains and is about to die, for I have not found your works complete in the sight of my God." -Revelation 3:2 ESV

How many beautiful, historic church buildings have been sold off and turned into yoga studios, art galleries, and pubs? Sacred spaces around the world are being stripped down and robbed of their divine purpose. Regardless of the circumstances, the fault almost always rests on pastors who insist upon having full control over everything, until there's nothing left to covet.

They want to have their cake and eat it too, but I think the one who endures to the end will be saved. (Matthew 24:13) You have been blessed to be a blessing, and the stakes are too high for a leisurely, early retirement. The younger generations aren't always easy to work with but it's time for the older generation to stop hoarding wealth, power, control, and influence.

It's time to stop living in luxury while the orphan, the widow, the prisoner, and the foreigner are lonely and struggling to put food on the table. Beloved, please don't fatten your heart on the day of slaughter. (James ch 5) If you're still alive, you have not endured to the end. If you're close to the finish line of life, the last thing you should do is give up.

No matter how small your circle of influence may be, please don't let your lamp go out. As far as it depends on you, make an effort to mentor a few disciples and trust the Lord for an increase. Please pass the torch to the next generation before it's too late. Before we move on, let's take a moment to thank God for the people in our lives. We all stumble in many ways, so it's important that we give each other a bit more grace. Reconciliation can begin with you, so don't wait for the other person to say sorry.

Chapter 22

Lukewarm "Laodicean" idols

"Peacemaking is not avoiding conflict. Running from a problem, pretending it doesn't exist, or being afraid to talk about it is actually cowardice. Jesus, the Prince of Peace, was never afraid of conflict. On occasion, he provoked it for the good of everyone." -Rick Warren

"Jesus entered the temple and drove out all who sold and bought in the temple, and he overturned the 'My house shall be called a house of prayer,' but you make it a den of robbers."
-Matthew 21:12-17 ESV

I'd like to share my thoughts on a few personal

experiences, but before we begin, please understand that I love Christian conferences and music festivals. There are tons of major events every year, and there's no way anyone could attend half of them. I can only speak about the ones I know, and I long to see our focus shift away from consumerism and the unintentional worship of Christian celebrities. Yes, even the most spiritual people, places, and things can be an idol if we aren't diligent.

Most of these special events do a great job of fostering unity among Christians, and that's why their importance cannot be understated. My passion for every flavor of interdenominational gatherings has led me to question a few trends, but before we begin, I should also say it's never God's will for us to become professional heresy hunters (read: busybodies) who run around gossiping, slandering, and looking for trouble instead of laboring in the harvest.

It's important that we defend the sanctity of large Christian gatherings, which are   sacred assemblies. Christians have lost the Jewish heritage of Christ including the feasts. There's nothing religious about celebrating Jewish holidays. I wish every Christian would take the time to understand their importance.

Christian conferences have unintentionally replaced those ancient festivals, and while it isn't the same thing, it's better than nothing. Festivals and conferences are a massive undertaking that requires a ton of work and planning. They aren't cheap, and thousands of hard-working people take off work briefly to pursue the Lord and to fellowship.

Apart from concerts, my favorite events are non-denominational and Charismatic conferences. I've been to many events where I encountered the sweet presence of the Lord in powerful ways. I love meeting and reconnecting with like-minded believers from around the world. When I've been at my lowest points in life Christian events helped jump-start my soul and remind me that I'm not alone.

To me, powerfully anointed conferences are about as close to Heaven as I can get. It's OK if you feel closer to the Lord in nature or other settings, but for me, these are true Kairos moments and a refreshing oasis. If you don't currently make time for multi-day Christian events, I urge you to reconsider. Please set aside a few weeks or weekends every year and remember that feasting is commanded more than fasting in the Old Testament!

You've probably noticed that Christian conferences and music festivals often feature popup book stores and various booths to sell all kinds of merchandise. Those can be helpful most of the time, but in some circles, humble, helpful book stores and coffee shops have grown to become consumeristic madhouses. Sacred assemblies should never become a den of robbers.

I'll never forget the time I wandered into a Christian conference in Dallas Texas. I won't disclose the name or specific location of this event because this isn't a personal attack it's a general observation about current trends. The event was held near the peak of the Great Recession in 2009.

The economy was terrible, millions of hard working families had recently lost their homes, major layoffs were happening all the time and tons of companies were going out of business. It was so bad that most newspapers removed their real estate section entirely.

The conference took place at a beautiful, elegant facility, but the bizarre bazaar of vendors and merchants made the place look and feel like a flea market. As soon as I walked in the door I was hit by a strong smell of shrink wrap and plastic. Anyone who's worked in retail knows what I'm talking about.

Folding tables and hanging racks overflowed with tall piles of cheap, cliché religious gifts, books, and polyester clothing. Vendors were hawking everything from tacky jewelry and bedazzled crosses to engraved wooden wall signs and bumper stickers. Almost everything there was a textbook example of planned obsolescence. Hardly anything looked like it was built to last.

There were rows of embroidered purses, fancy hats, and cowboy boots festooned with large colorful crosses. It was everything you never wanted and more. For a few moments, I stood still, dumbfounded by the sad scene unfolding in front of my eyes. Hundreds of affluent, overweight, middle-aged ladies were lining up to buy overpriced ornaments while talking about themselves.

I hate to put it so bluntly, and I'm sorry if this offends you, but that's what I say. God will judge me for everything I say and I don't take this lightly. The idols of greed, vanity, and self-indulgence were worshipped under the guise of Christianity and it made me sick to my stomach. "Take care, and be on your guard against all covetousness, for one's life does not consist in the abundance of his possessions." -Luke 12:15 ESV

Vast amounts of territory have been lost and forfeited by believers because the risk of offense is valued over righteous living and holiness. We've taken the focus off Jesus and put it squarely on ourselves, but there's no amount of self help that can replace Christ's call to radical selflessness. Polite Christians are too busy affirming each other while remaining passive in the face of evil.

The organizers of this particular conference in 2009 turned God's temple (a large church) into a den of robbers. To add insult to injury, major events like this always feature a few prominent guest speakers to give lend it some credibility, and the ruse works like a charm. Highly trusted Christian celebrities are leading the way with this defiling, inglorious trend. Has the glory departed from your favorite Christian events? (1 Samuel 4:2, Matthew 23:37–38)

As I walked down the aisles of this consumeristic conference, I couldn't help but think of the persecuted church around the world. Wealthy churchgoers wander around aimlessly and practice their networking skills while

Christians in hostile nations are tortured and murdered just for owning a Bible. The marketplace ministry is only valid if you're actively engaging in or directly financing the ministry. Jesus gives seed to the sower, and He hasn't forgotten about you. If you don't feel like you're receiving your share of seed money, then take a long hard look at your personal finances.

"You say, 'I am rich; I have grown wealthy and need nothing.' But you do not realize that you are wretched, pitiful, poor, blind, and naked. I counsel you to buy from Me gold refined by fire so that you may become rich, white garments so that you may be clothed and your shameful nakedness not exposed, and salve to anoint your eyes so that you may see. Those I love, I rebuke and discipline. Therefore be earnest and repent" -Revelation 3:17-19 BSB

"Christ has come to free us from idolatry to sin so that we might serve God out of gratitude for the grace that He has bestowed upon us. Christ is the only one who has ever kept the first commandment and loved God with all of his heart, soul, mind, and strength. Christ Jesus died under the curse of the Law for idolaters who repent and believe the Gospel of grace." -Martin Luther

I walked away from the shop-until-you-drop Christian conference after about ten or fifteen minutes, but it troubled me for days afterward. On my way out I saw a promotional flyer for the event, which boasted about Christian virtues. All I could do was shake my head and sigh as I left the building.

Please believe that I'm not trying to be "holier than thou" with my observations. God is always working, even in the worst circumstances, but that doesn't mean we should blindly accept everything that's labeled as Christian without raising questions or legitimate concerns.

Some will claim that a conferences isn't a church,

even when it's are hosted in a church or a Christian University, but that opinion ignores the fact that these events use the Gospel (and their association with Christian celebrities) to sell tickets and booth spaces. They talk about spiritual enlightenment while making every effort to blur the lines of what is acceptable as they piggyback off our gullible, conflicted nature. We desire the weighty, spiritual things of God while simultaneously falling for gimmicks, false advertising, and marketing ploys.

If the event I attended was honestly advertised as a pseudo flea market, there wouldn't be an issue and I would've gone somewhere else that day. We must hold Christian events to the standards they have announced in public. Church happens whenever two or more gather in the name of Jesus (Matthew 18:20). We are turning the temple into a den of thieves and trading eternal treasures of gold for worthless, plastic trinkets. It's time to stop the madness.

The mark of the beast (Revelation 13:16) will directly impact our ability to buy and sell. If you refuse to take the mark you will be barred from shopping in public and your business will be destroyed or confiscated. The same thing happened to the Jews during the Holocaust. The mark of the beast is inextricably linked to buying and selling and God will allow this to test your heart.

What will you do when you can't legally buy or sell anything without first worshipping the devil and taking his mark on your body? Will you run and hide in the mountains, or try to get what you need under the table, in the black market? There won't be a lot of options. A line is being drawn in the sand, and if you're still stuck in idolatry when that day comes, your odds of survival won't be good.

If you're sold out for Jesus and walking with Him, you will stand strong and take courage, knowing that God makes a way for those who love Him. When this terrible day comes, and it's coming soon, we will see cultural Christians standing in line to take the mark because they never learned to fear the Lord. They only ever loved what God could do for them. Just Esau in Genesis, billions of souls will scorn their eternal inheritance for the sake of convenience.

The next time you think about buying your dog a steak, I hope you'll buy one for a kid whose struggling to hold onto his faith, like a sheep without a shepherd. Some of those young men and women have never been to a nice restaurant. Maybe you could take them out for lunch or invite them to your home for dinner.

I believe God cares about the things we value, and just like any good Father, He wants us to have fun and to be successful. Our creator has emotions and He imparted those to us when He breathed life into our bodies. Every good gift comes from above and that includes sports, recreation, and your family pet. God the Father has good plans for your life, to prosper you and not harm you.

So stay on the narrow road and walk with Him. Never give up and be encouraged no matter how many times you fail. Pray for your enemies and bless those who curse you. Finally, be anxious for nothing (Philippians 4:6) and always remember that two stray dogs are sold for a penny, but you are worth more than many Schnauzers.

P.S. If you're thinking about taking a whip into a Christian conference, and driving anyone out, please don't do it! Instead, let's learn to love our enemies and choose to live by these words of wisdom: "Do not repay anyone evil for evil; be concerned for what is noble in the sight of all. If possible, on your part, live at peace with all. Beloved, do not look for revenge but leave room for the wrath; for it is written, "Vengeance is mine, I will repay, says the Lord." Rather, "if your enemy is hungry, feed him; if he is thirsty, give him something to drink; for by so doing you will heap burning coals upon his head." Do not be conquered by evil but conquer evil with good." -Romans 12:17-21 NASB

For more information please contact us at:
Mistretta Ministries
briomichael@gmail.com
310-926-7571

Social media
@xerofly for the following apps;
Instagram, Facebook, Twitter, Periscope, Venmo, PayPal,
Cash App...

(1) Younggren, Jeffrey N.; Boisvert, Jennifer A.; Boness, Cassandra L. (August 2016). "Examining Emotional Support Animals and Role Conflicts in Professional Psychology". Professional Psychology: Research and Practice.

(2)
    McCune, Sandra; Esposito, Layla; Griffin, James A. (2017-02-23). "Introduction to a thematic   series on animal assisted interventions in special populations". Applied Developmental Science.

(3)
    Crossman, Molly K. (2016-11-03). "Effects of Interactions With Animals On Human   Psychological Distress". Journal of Clinical Psychology.

(4)
    Jacobson–Brulliard, Karin (2 July 2017). "Therapy animals are everywhere. Proof that they help   is not". Washington Post.

(5)
https://onlinelibrary.wiley.com/doi/abs/10.1002/jclp.22410

(6) "Missions encompass more than evangelism, but evangelism is the heart of missions. Programs, buildings, new organs and more staff aren't misplaced if there are higher priorities with proportionate budgets... Churches can become like tired corporations—having lost their sense of purpose and accompanying zeal, they focus upon form, risk-avoidance and status-quo bureaucracy." -Jim Sutherland

(7) Barrett, David B., Todd M. Johnson, and Peter F. Crossing. 2005. Missiometrics 2005: A global survey of world mission. International Bulletin of Missionary Research 29 (January): 29. This includes nominal Christians.

(8) Barna, George. "Stewardship" http://www.barna.org/FlexPage.aspx?Page=Topic&TopicID=36 accessed 3/23/05

(9) Barna, George. 2004. "Religious beliefs remain constant but subgroups are quite different" http://www.barna.org/FlexPage.aspx?Page=BarnaUpdate&BarnaUpdateID=160 accessed 3/23/05.

(10) More than half of donors (55%) say they donated an amount of $500 or less. Specifically, roughly one in five (22%) noted the total value of their donations as $100 or less, while 33% gave between $100 and $500, 20% donated a total value of $500 up to $1,000, 12% contributed between $1,000 and $2,500, 8% offered $2,500 up to $5,000, and 5% estimated their donated total as more than $5,000... The research shows that 5% of adults

qualify as having tithed—giving 10% or more of their annual income to a church or non-profit organizations. In 2009, before the financial crisis, tithing was 7%, then dipped to 4% in 2010 and 2011. (Note: Barna calculates this "tithing" rate based on total giving divided by household income, not by asking survey respondents to estimate percentages.) Among born again Christians, which includes both evangelicals and non-evangelicals, 12% tithed in 2012, which is on par with the average for the past decade.

(11)   https://www.washingtonpost.com/news/wonk/wp/2015/02/11/big-pharmaceutical-companies-are-spending-far-more-on-marketing-than-research/

(12)   https://www.nerdwallet.com/blog/health/medical-bankruptcy/

(13)   International Human Rights Law on Solitary Confinement, HRF, 2015.pdf

(14)   https://www.theguardian.com/world/2018/jan/24/saudi-camel-beauty-contest-judges-get--hump-botox-cheats

(15)   http://www.dailytelegraph.com.au/news/nsw/news-story/3d45e451862a9873d3ae506afdcd8458

(16)   https://lifehacker.com/change-your-screen-to-grayscale-to-combat-phone-addicti-1795821843

(17)   https://www.theatlantic.com/business/archive/2016/01/lottery-winners-research/423543/

(18)   https://www.businessinsider.com/these-6-corporations-control-90-of-the-media-in-america-2012-6

(19)   https://www.freetheslaves.net/our-

model-for-freedom/slavery-today/

(20)   https://www.apologeticspress.org/apcontent.aspx?category=11&article=2407

CPSIA information can be obtained
at www.ICGtesting.com
Printed in the USA
BVHW031418160223
658652BV00003B/32